OF DEMOCRATS & DICTATORS

The Development of Law

From Elizabethan England to the Modern Age

CRF
Constitutional Rights Foundation
Educating Tomorrow's Citizens

OF DEMOCRATS & DICTATORS
The Development of Law

Developed by

Marshall Croddy
Bill Hayes

Writers

Bill Hayes
Carlton Martz
Marshall Croddy

Editor

Bill Hayes

Production & Design

Andrew Costly

Todd Clark, Executive Director
Marshall Croddy, Director of Programs
Constitutional Rights Foundation
601 South Kingsley Drive
Los Angeles, CA 90005
(213) 487-5590
crf@crf-usa.org • www.crf-usa.org

Library of Congress Cataloging-in-Publication Data

Croddy, Marshall.

Of democrats & dictators: the development of law / developed by Marshall Croddy, Bill Hayes ; writers, Marshall Croddy, Bill Hayes, Carlton Martz ; editor, Bill Hayes.

p. cm.

Includes bibliographical references.

ISBN 1-886253-39-0 (alk. paper)

1. Law–History. I. Hayes, Bill, 1945-II. Martz, Carlton S., 1940-III. Title. IV. Title: Of democrats and dictators.

K150.C76 2007

340.09–dc22

2007000995

OF DEMOCRATS & DICTATORS

The Development of Law

From Elizabethan England to the Modern Age

Unit 1: Sir Edward Coke and the Common Law 6

Unit 2: The Enlightenment Philosophers 30

Unit 3: The Code Napoleon 40

Unit 4: The Dreyfus Affair 58

Unit 5: The Totalitarians 70

Unit 6: War Crimes 90

Unit 7: Gandhi and Civil Disobedience 100

Unit 8: International Law 108

Bibliography 123

Of Democrats & Dictators
The Development of Law

From the Elizabethan England to the Modern Age

Detailed Table of Contents

Unit 1: Sir Edward Coke and the Common Law **6**

The Rise of the Common Law 6

Inns of Court 9

The Evolution of the Jury System 10

The Trial of Sir Walter Raleigh 12

Coke on the Bench 14

The Court of Chancery 17

The Case of the Five Knights 21

The Petition of Right 23

Later Developments in Common Law 27

Unit 2: The Enlightenment Philosophers **30**

The Enlightenment 30

Thomas Hobbes 32

John Locke 33

Baron de Montesquieu 35

Jean-Jacques Rousseau 36

Unit 3: The Code Napoleon **40**

The French Revolution 40

Napoleon 44

The Law in France Before the Code 45

Making the Code 46

The Civil Code 50

The Code's Legacy 54

Differences Between the Civil Code and Common Law 55

Unit 4: The Dreyfus Affair **58**

The Arrest and Court-Martial 58

A Press War Erupts 61

The Unraveling of the Case 64

Dreyfus' Second Court-Martial 65

The End of the Affair 67

Unit 5: The Totalitarians **70**
The Rise of Totalitarian States in Germany and Russia 70
The Stalin Purges 73
The Terror 74
The Show Trials 76
Hitler's Rise to Total Power 78
Reichstag Fire Trial 79
Nazi "Justice" 81
The Plot to Assassinate Hitler 85
The Hitler Plot Trials 87

Unit 6: War Crimes **90**
The Hague Conventions 90
The Nuremberg Tribunal 93
The International Criminal Court 96

Unit 7: Gandhi and Civil Disobedience **100**
A Brief History of India 100
Gandhi's Early Years 102
Gandhi Against the Empire 104
Independence and Assassination 106

Unit 8: International Law **108**
A Brief History of International Law 108
What Is International Law? 111
Law of the Sea 114
Piracy 116
A Treaty to Control the Spread of Nuclear Weapons 118

Bibliography **123**

Unit 1

Sir Edward Coke and the Common Law

In 1066, William of Normandy defeated Harold II, the English king, at the Battle of Hastings. This is a section of the Bayeux Tapestry, which depicts the Norman conquest. The tapestry, created within years of the battle, measures 20 inches by 230 feet.

The Rise of the Common Law

The English common law is one of the two great systems of law in the Western world. The other is the French Civil Code. The common law exists in England and in those countries that were once its colonies—the United States, Canada, Australia, New Zealand, India, and other countries. Much of the rest of the world uses law based on the French Civil Code.

The Civil Code was enacted in France in 1804. All the law is written in one book. The common law is based on the decisions of judges in individual cases. The law grew slowly, case by case. It is judge-made law.

The common law began shortly after A.D. 1066, the date of the Norman conquest of England. William, the Duke of Normandy, crossed the channel from France and became king of England. He appointed his judges to the already-existing courts of the Anglo-Saxons. The German Anglo-Saxons themselves had conquered the land six centuries earlier.

The Anglo-Saxon courts featured trial by oath and trial by ordeal. In a trial by oath, the two disputing parties would gather as many people as

Vocabulary

accusatorial system (ə KŪZ ə tor ē əl SIS təm) n. Also known as the adversary system. In this system of justice, the two opposing parties present evidence. A judge runs the trial but does not investigate the case or otherwise play an active role.

barrister (BÄR ə stər) n. A member of the bar; an attorney permitted to try cases in court. (Used in Britain.)

capital offense (KAP ə təl ə FENS) n. A crime punishable by death.

cause of action (KOZ UV AK shən) n. The facts that give rise to a legal basis to sue.

contempt of court (kən TEMPT UV KORT) n. Showing disrespect for the court or failing to follow a court order. Punishable by a fine or jail time.

cross-examine (KROS ig ZAM in) v. To question the other party's witness in court.

demurrer (də MER ər) n. An objection that a pleading does not state a cause of action recognized by the law.

equity (EK wi tē) n. A system of justice parallel to the common law. Developed by the Court of Chancery, it was based on principles of good faith and fair dealing derived from Roman law.

grand jury (GRAND JER ē) n. A group of citizens responsible for determining whether the prosecution has enough evidence against a defendant to justify holding a trial. It meets in secret, and the prosecutor presents evidence to it.

habeas corpus (HĀ bē əs COR pəs) n. A writ, or court order, for the executive (police, prosecutors, prison officials) to produce a prisoner in court and justify the legality of the imprisonment. (Latin for "you have the body.")

indictment (in DĪT mənt) n. A grand jury's formal charge against a defendant confirming that sufficient evidence exists to justify holding a trial.

injunction (in JUNK shən) n. A court order telling a party to refrain from doing something or to perform a specific action.

Magna Carta (MAG nə CAR tə) n. Written in 1215, it is one of England's most important documents enshrining liberty. (Latin meaning "great charter.")

maxim (MAK sim) n. A basic principle or rule.

parchment (PARCH mənt) n. A sheet made from sheep or goat skin to write or paint on.

perjury (PER jə rē) n. The act of lying under oath; telling a lie or misleading someone when you have sworn to tell the truth.

plaintiff (PLĀN tf) n. The party suing the defendant in a lawsuit.

pleading (PLĒD i*ng*) n. The formal statement, usually written, spelling out the plaintiff's or defendant's case to the court.

precedent (PRES i dənt) n. An issue of law previously decided by a court that other courts must follow.

proclamation (prok lə MĀ shən) n. An official announcement.

Raleigh (ROL ē) Sir Walter Raleigh (1554–1618), English explorer, soldier, and writer.

subpoena (sə PĒ nə) n. An order to appear in court to testify. (Latin for "under penalty.")

tort (TORT) n. A wrongful act (other than breach of contract) that serves as the basis for a lawsuit. The wrongful act usually must be done intentionally or negligently.

Tower of London (TOW er UV LUN dən) A fortress in London used as a jail for important prisoners.

Pronunciation Key: bat, **ā**te, **ar**e, d**ä**re, den, **ē**go, **new**, h**er**, bit, **ī**ce, **î**rritate, b**o**x, n**ō**, b**or**n, **oi**l, **ou**t, b**u**t, **ū**se, **ch**um, **sh**e, **th**in, ***th**e*, **zh** sound in trea**s**ure or mira**g**e; **ə** is the **uh** sound in unaccented syllables.

possible to swear that their side was right. In a trial by ordeal, a person charged with a crime would undergo a test. For example, the person might have to hold a hot iron. If after three days the wound healed, the person was innocent. If it didn't heal, the person was guilty.

The Normans tried to centralize justice in the kingdom by sending out judges from the king's courts. They traveled on circuits, dispensing justice. Gradually, these courts replaced all the Anglo-Saxon courts. These were the courts of the common law, the law common to all of England.

As it took shape, the common law had three defining characteristics. One was the jury system. The Normans brought a primitive form of the jury system with them. Over time, it developed into two kinds of juries. One was the jury of 12 members, which heard evidence and gave a verdict in a trial. The other was the grand jury, which heard evidence to determine whether there was enough evidence to try someone for a crime. If it found sufficient evidence, it issued an indictment.

Another feature of the common law was the accusatorial system. The judge acted like a referee in court between two battling parties. The judge did not conduct an investigation. The parties had to present the evidence.

The final main characteristic of the common law was precedent. Once a court decided a case, it made law. The court should follow its prior decisions and the decisions of higher courts. Such a system required that judges and lawyers know about other decisions. This knowledge gradually became available through treatises on law and reports on cases.

Thousands of people built the common law. One of the most important was Sir Edward Coke—lawyer, judge, and member of Parliament. Many people who knew him considered him arrogant and narrow. He lived in Elizabethan England. Yet he never attended a play by Shakespeare or any other playwright. He knew little outside his main focus—the common law.

English historian George M. Trevelyan called Coke "one of the most disagreeable figures in our history" and also "one of the most important champions of our liberty." Coke lived at a pivotal time in England's history. King James and his successor, King Charles, were asserting their right to rule absolutely. Parliament was challenging the king's power. Coke began his career advocating for the monarchy. He ended it advocating that everyone, including the king, should be under the rule of law.

For Discussion

1. Who were the Normans? What were trials like before the Normans came to England?

2. What is the common law? What are its three main characteristics?

3. From what you've read in this article, how is the common law different from the French Civil Code?

Inns of Court

An 1830 drawing of Lincoln's Inn, one of the four Inns of Court. The inns had the exclusive authority to train lawyers.

Edward Coke was born in 1552 in Norfolk, a county in eastern England. His father was a lawyer, and Coke also wanted to practice law. He attended Cambridge University and then went to the Inner Temple, one of the so-called Inns of Court.

In 1291, King Edward I had ordered that only a select few could serve as lawyers before the king's courts. Within a few years, the Inns of Court were established for training lawyers. They were located within walking distance of the king's courts at Westminster Hall in London. Students lived, studied, and debated with one another at the inns. They often attended court to watch lawyers in action. The inns had the exclusive authority to grant someone permission to practice law in court. (This was known as calling someone to the bar.)

Coke threw himself into studying law. The course of study lasted typically eight years. One of the things that law students studied was Year Books. These recorded the decisions and arguments in the king's courts. They were created each year from 1291 to 1535. They were so detailed that they often captured exchanges between judges and attorneys. The Year Books helped lawyers cite previous court decisions in their arguments. By Coke's time, legal arguments were long and filled with citations of court decisions.

Around 1500, more formal case reports started replacing the Year Books. These were like today's case reports, showing the decisions of the cases and the reasoning of the judges. They did not report on the back and forth arguments in the courtroom. Coke at the end of his career wrote 11 volumes of case reports, commenting on the common law. The case books helped the common law's practice of relying on precedent, the rulings in previous cases.

Like other law students, Coke studied legal treatises. One was *De legibus et consuetudinibus Angliae* (on the laws and customs of England). It was written in Latin by Henri de Bracton (1215–1268), a judge on Court of Common Pleas. Bracton retrieved the decisions of cases recorded on rolls of parchment. He wrote down the decisions and reasoning of 2,000 cases. Also a priest, Bracton classified the decisions according to the categories of Roman law. One conclusion of Bracton deeply influenced Coke: The king must bow to God and the common law.

Students also studied pleading. The common law required different writs (court orders) for each cause of action. For example, to sue for breach of contract required one type of writ. To sue someone who stole a pig required another. Each writ gave rise to different procedures, which made the common law difficult to understand.

Originally, pleading was done orally in front of the court. The plaintiff stated his version of the facts of the case. If these facts failed to state a cause of action, the case was dismissed. If they did state one, then the defendant was supposed to answer. He could deny the facts or assert a special defense. Once the judge settled the pleading, court clerks recorded them on parchment. The pleadings framed the issues of fact for the jury to decide.

By Coke's time, paper had replaced the far more expensive parchment, and the pleadings were done on paper instead of orally. The plaintiff wrote the facts in a complaint, and the defendant responded with a written answer. If the defendant believed the facts in the complaint did not state a cause of action, he could file what was known as a demurrer. The court would then rule on the demurrer.

Pleading was complex and could have serious consequences on a case. If, for example, the written pleading differed from the proof offered at trial, the case would be dismissed.

When Coke was called to the bar in 1578, he was one of just 200 lawyers in all of England. An advocate needed to know three languages. One was Norman French. The Year Books until 1400 were published in that language. Another was Latin, because the court record was written in it. The third was English, which the clients spoke and which had become in Coke's time the language for arguing in court (replacing Norman French).

The members of the bar were known as barristers. After 16 to 20 years of practice, a barrister could be named a serjeant-at-law, a senior member of the bar. From the serjeants-at-law, the king picked the judges of his courts.

For Discussion

1. How did a person become a lawyer in Coke's time? How is it different today in America?
2. What was the course of study at one of the Inns of Court? Based on what you know about law school in the United States today, how is the course of study different in the United States?
3. What is pleading? How was it done in Coke's day?
4. What statement of Bracton deeply influenced Coke? What does this statement mean? Do you agree with it? Explain.

The Evolution of the Jury System

Coke returned to Norfolk to begin practicing law. He quickly earned a reputation as a great trial lawyer. One case gained him fame throughout England. It was *Wolfe v. Shelley*, and as every law student today knows, it established the *Rule in Shelley's Case.* Although the case involved a technical issue of land law, it drew great attention throughout England. The queen felt the issue so important that she directed all the judges on the Queen's Bench to meet to hear the case. When Coke won the case, he was looked on as one of the best lawyers in the land.

Coke's success got the attention of the queen. In 1592, Queen Elizabeth named him solicitor general. The following year, he was elevated to attorney general, the government's top attorney.

During Coke's term as attorney general, he worked tirelessly for the interests of the monarch, first Queen Elizabeth and then her successor, James I.

James disliked Parliament intensely. Referring to Parliament, James once remarked: "I am surprised that my ancestors should ever have allowed such an institution to come into existence." James wanted to assume absolute power in the kingdom. Coke as attorney general assisted him in his efforts.

Coke prosecuted a series of libel cases against those who had insulted the crown. Most notable, however, were several high-profile treason cases he pursued. One of the most famous was the Gunpowder Plot. A group of Catholic radicals, distressed about how members of their religion were treated, had planned to blow up Parliament and the new king. One of the plotters, Guy Fawkes, was captured on November 5, 1606. This date is still celebrated in England with bonfires, fireworks, and burned effigies of Fawkes. Fawkes was prosecuted by Coke, convicted, and executed.

A sketch of the members of the Gunpowder Plot. Guy Fawkes is third from the right.

The Jury

All of Coke's trials took place before a jury. The Normans had introduced jury trials to England, and jury trials were an important part of the common law. But the first juries were far different from those of today. Twelve upstanding men were selected to serve on a jury. No lawyers spoke to the jury. No witnesses testified. The members of the jury were both witnesses and investigators. They could go out and seek information, or they could rely on what they already knew. In the early days, most trials involved questions of land. The only way land could be transferred was by an elaborate public ceremony or by the owner dying. The members of the jury would normally have firsthand knowledge of the facts necessary to transfer land.

Even after legal questions became more complex and less likely to be within the knowledge of jurors, the common law did not allow jurors to hear testimony. One reason for this resistance may have been the legal practices of the Anglo-Saxons. In most of their trials, the two sides gathered witnesses who swore under oath that their side was right. These "swearing contests" resulted in mass perjury, deliberate false testimony under oath. For years, the common law avoided using witnesses out of fear of perjury.

By Coke's day, however, the fear had lessened, and the jury had evolved. It no longer was expected to know the facts of the case. It was to base its verdict on evidence presented in court. Much of this evidence was testimony from witnesses. But no rules evidence had yet been established. That meant that the prosecutor could introduce any evidence he wanted—hearsay, rumor, speculation.

For Discussion

1. How did Coke's career progress?
2. What was King James' attitude toward Parliament? How did Coke assist King James?
3. What were the first juries like? How had they changed by Coke's time? What caused the resistance to letting juries hear testimony?
4. What are some rules of evidence that courts have today? Why do you think modern courts have these rules? Do you think these rules are necessary or should attorneys be able to present whatever evidence they like? Explain.

The Trial of Sir Walter Raleigh

Coke's most famous (and notorious) trial was of Sir Walter Raleigh in 1603. Raleigh was an explorer, soldier, and writer. He was a favorite at the court of Queen Elizabeth. But her successor, James, distrusted him.

The king's Privy Council, a group of royal advisors, charged Raleigh with high treason. It was alleged that he had plotted with his friend, Lord Cobham, to foment rebellion and to get Arabella Stuart of Spain put on the throne of England instead of James, the king of Scotland. Hints were made that Arabella would be sympathetic to the Roman Catholic Church. But both Raleigh and Arabella were Protestants. His alleged involvement in a plot with Spain was particularly dubious. Raleigh had always favored an aggressive policy against Spain.

Raleigh was arrested and put in the Tower of London. After a few weeks, guards took him to the town of Winchester, a ride of several days from London. His trial was held there.

He was not told of the charges against him. They were first read to him at the beginning of his trial. He pleaded not guilty.

Raleigh had no attorney. A person on trial for a capital offense could not have an attorney.

Raleigh told the court that his memory was bad, and he asked permission to respond to the charges as they were made, instead of waiting to the end of the case. Coke objected, saying that the prosecution's case would lose its force if it were "broken or dismembered." The court, however, granted Raleigh's request.

Coke began his opening statement. He talked about other treason cases and gave examples of treason. Then he accused Raleigh of wanting to harm the king's children.

Surprised at the charge, Raleigh blurted out, "To whom speak you this? You tell me news I never heard of."

Coke prosecuted Sir Walter Raleigh (c. 1554–1618) for treason in 1603.

Coke replied, "Oh, sir, do I? I will prove you to be the most notorious traitor that ever came to the bar. . . ."

Raleigh countered, "Your words cannot condemn me. My innocence is my defense. . . . Prove against me any one thing of the many . . . and I will confess all of the indictment . . . ."

Coke responded, "Nay, I will prove all: thou art a monster. Thou hast an English face but a Spanish heart."

In fact, Coke offered little evidence of Raleigh's guilt. Raleigh was not allowed to call witnesses or to cross-examine the witnesses against him. Such was the practice in capital trials. Few witnesses appeared in person. Coke, the prosecutor, read witnesses' statements to the jury.

Throughout the trial, Coke continued to heap abuse on Raleigh, insulting him. Among other names, he called Raleigh "odious," "a viper," "the absolutest traitor that ever was," and "Machiavellian and devilish."

Raleigh was not rattled. He kept asking for proof.

The most damaging piece of evidence was an unsigned written statement from his friend Lord Cobham. It said that Raleigh was the instigator of the plot.

Raleigh demanded to confront his accuser, who was imprisoned nearby:

> I claim to have my accuser brought here face to face to speak. The Proof of the Common Law is by witnesses and jury: Let Cobham be here, let him speak it. If you proceed to condemn me by bare inferences, without an oath, without subscription, upon a paper accusation, you try me by the Spanish Inquisition. . . . If Cobham will maintain his accusation to my face, I will confess myself guilty.

The court denied this demand.

Coke read a letter from Cobham, again accusing Raleigh of leading the plot. But Raleigh took out another letter from Cobham, written from prison and secretly sent to Raleigh. It denied that Raleigh had anything to do with the plot.

The case went to the jury, which took only 15 minutes to find Raleigh guilty. He was sentenced to death, but the sentence was not carried out right away. He was taken to the Tower of London and released after 13 years. In 1618, however, the king had him rearrested, and Raleigh was executed under the original sentence.

Coke had earned a victory but at great cost to his reputation. More than 100 years later, the great English Chief Justice William Murray stated, "I would not have made Coke's speech in Sir Walter Raleigh's case to gain all of Coke's estate and reputation." The article on Coke in the *Encyclopaedia Britannica* concludes that Coke's methods "were brutal even by 17th-century standards." Other historians, however, contend that Coke's behavior was like that of other prosecutors of his day.

For Discussion

1. What was the charge against Raleigh? What evidence did the prosecution have against him?
2. Do you think Raleigh had a fair trial? Explain.

ACTIVITY

Appeal

Although many at the time thought Sir Walter Raleigh's trial was unfair, he was tried according to then-existing law. A criminal defendant's due-process rights would later develop more fully in England and in the United States.

Imagine that Raleigh's trial had taken place today in the United States. You are his attorney and must prepare a legal brief, a written argument, stating which of his rights under the U.S. Constitution were violated. The appeal will be heard by a federal appeals court.

When you write your brief, refer to the facts of Raleigh's case. Go through the Fifth and Sixth Amendments to the U.S. Constitution, listed below. These amendments are the main sources of the due-process rights that criminal defendants have in the United States. Find as many violations of Raleigh's rights as you can.

In your brief, write a separate paragraph for each violation. Tell exactly what happened to Raleigh in his trial, what specific right this violated, and why.

Fifth Amendment

No person shall be held to answer for a capital, or otherwise infamous crime, unless on a presentment or indictment of a Grand Jury, except in cases arising in the land or naval forces, or in the Militia, when in actual service in time of War or public danger; nor shall any person be subject of the same offence to be twice put in jeopardy of life or limb; nor shall be compelled in any criminal case to be a witness against himself, nor be deprived of life, liberty, or property, without due process of law; nor shall private property be taken for public use, without just compensation.

Sixth Amendment

In all criminal prosecutions, the accused shall enjoy the right to a speedy and public trial, by an impartial jury of the State and district wherein the crime shall have been committed, which district shall have been previously ascertained by law, and to be informed of the nature and cause of the accusation; to be confronted with the witnesses against him; to have compulsory process for obtaining Witnesses in his favor, and to have the Assistance of Counsel for his defence.

Coke on the Bench

In 1606, King James honored Coke for his years of service by naming him chief justice of the Court of Common Pleas. Coke was not a serjeant-at-law, and the king could only pick judges from the serjeants-at-law. So Coke was named a serjeant-at-law on the same day he was made chief justice.

James expected Coke to continue serving royal power as he had done as attorney general. The king was deeply mistaken. James sought absolute power as monarch, but Coke became an outspoken advocate of the rule of law and a champion of the common-law courts. He opposed the king by trying to make the common-law courts more powerful and to keep them independent of the king.

One of Coke's first targets was the Court of High Commission, a church court. Coke believed the court was taking cases that belonged in the common-law courts. He, and judges at his urging, began issuing writs of prohibition, ordering the Court of High Commission to hand over jurisdiction of particular cases.

James, as king, was head of the church. Church officials complained to the king about Coke and the other judges. In November 1608, the king called a meeting of the judges. The head of the Church of England, the archbishop of Canterbury, spoke. He wanted Coke to stop interfering with the church's courts. In his argument, he stated that the king could decide any case:

> The judges are but delegates of Your Majesty and administer the law in your name. What may be done by the agent may be done by the principal.

All the judges agreed except Coke. He answered the archbishop saying that "the king in his own person cannot adjudge any case . . . but this ought to be determined and adjudged in some court of justice, according to the law and custom of England."

Sir Edward Coke (1552–1634) was one of the most important legal thinkers in the history of the common law.

King James responded. Referring to Coke's maxim that "the common law is nothing but reason," the king said:

> I always thought . . . that your English law was founded upon reason. If that be so, why have not I and others reason as well as you, the judges?

Coke agreed that the king was fully capable of reasoning. But he said:

> Your Majesty is not learned in the laws of . . . England, and causes which concern the life, or inheritance, or goods, or fortunes of your subjects, are not to be decided by natural reason, but by the artificial reason and judgment of law, which law is an art which requires long study and experience before that a man can attain to the cognizance of it. . . .

Angered, James thundered, "Then I am to be *under* the law—which it is treason to affirm."

Coke responded by citing Bracton, the author of one of the great treatises on the common law: "The king ought not to be under any man but under God and the law."

The king flew into a rage. Reportedly, Coke fell to his knees and begged the king's forgiveness. James left the meeting thinking Coke had submitted to him.

The next day, Coke issued another writ of prohibition ordering the Court of High Commission to turn over jurisdiction in a case. Coke continued his battle against the church court. In an attempt to end the conflict, the king even offered Coke a position as judge on the Court of High Commission. Coke turned him down.

Royal Proclamations

Neither the king nor Coke won a clear victory over the jurisdiction of the Court of High Commission. But in another area, Coke was the clear victor. King James had taken to issuing royal proclamations. All monarchs had issued them. But Coke pointed out that previous proclamations only made people of England aware of pre-existing law. King James believed he could make new law, even crimes, through proclamations.

Coke and Parliament disagreed with the king. In 1610, Parliament sent the king a petition objecting to making law through proclamations. The king responded by saying he would only do it in cases of emergency. That did not satisfy his critics.

The Privy Council, a group of the king's advisors, met to discuss proclamations. The group invited Coke to join the discussion. Coke's research showed that all past indictments had concluded "with the words, Against the law and custom of England . . . or against laws and statutes . . . ." None had concluded with the words "against the king's proclamation." Coke's arguments won the day. The council decided that:

> . . . the King by his proclamation cannot create any offence which was not an offence before . . . . [T]he law of England is divided into three Parts: Common Law, Statute Law, and Custom; but the King's Proclamation is none of them.

Excerpt From Part 12 of the *Reports* by Sir Edward Coke

Note, the King by his Proclamation, or other waies, cannot change any part of the Common Law, or Statute Law, or the Customs of the Realm . . . . Also the King cannot create any Offence by his Prohibition or Proclamation, which was not an Offence before, for that was to change the Law, and to make an Offence which was not, for *Ubi non est lex, ibi non est transgressio, ergo*, [Where there is no Law, there is no trespass; therefore] that which cannot be punished without proclamation, cannot be punished with it. . . .

But a thing which is punishable by the Law, by fine and imprisonment, if the King prohibit it by his Proclamation, before that he will punish it, and so warn his Subjects of the peril of it, there if he commit it after, this as a Circumstance aggravates the Offence; But he by Proclamation cannot make a thing unlawful, which was permitted by the Law before: And this was well proved by the ancient and continuall forms of Indictments, for all Indictments conclude, *Contra legem & consuetudinem Angliae* [Against the Law and custom of England], or *Contra leges & statuta,& c.* [Against the Laws and Statutes, etc.] but never was seen any Indictment to conclude *Contra Regiam proclamatonem* [Against the royal proclamation].

The King's Bench

In 1613, the king appointed Coke chief justice of the King's Bench and made him a member of his Privy Council. He thought putting Coke in these positions would make him indebted to him and less likely to interfere with his power. But the king was wrong.

Coke kept asserting the rule of common law over the king. In one case, the attorney general was unsure whether he could get a conviction if he prosecuted it. The attorney general went to the judges on the Court of the King's Bench and asked them whether they would convict the man, a Puritan preacher. Two judges told the prosecutor that they would. Coke refused. He stated that "judges ought not to deliver their opinions beforehand in any criminal case that may come before them judicially."

In another lawsuit, the king wrote the judges asking them to postpone the case. Under Coke's guidance, the judges wrote back that the law did not give the king this privilege. The king called all the judges to appear before him. All the judges, except Coke, said they were wrong.

The king asked, "In a case where the king believes his . . . interest concerned, . . . ought they not stay the proceedings till His Majesty has consulted them?"

They all answered yes. But Coke replied: "When the case happens, I shall do that which shall be fit for a judge to do."

For Discussion

1. What was the dispute about between King James and Coke over the Court of High Commission? In supporting the king's right to decide any case, the argument was made that "What may be done by the agent may be done by the principal." What does this statement mean? How did Coke respond to this statement? Do you agree with Coke? Explain.

2. What was the dispute about over royal proclamations? How was the dispute resolved? What would be the danger if the king's position had prevailed?

3. On the Court of the King's Bench, what were some problems Coke had with the king and his government? Do you think Coke was right to object to what the crown was doing? Explain.

4. In response to a question by the king, Coke stated: ". . . I shall do that which shall be fit for a judge to do." What do you think Coke believed it was fit for a judge to do? What do you think the king believed a judge should do? Who do you think was right? Why?

The Court of Chancery

The Court of Chancery is depicted in this early 19th-century drawing. The court arose to correct problems with the common law.

One of Coke's last battles as a judge dealt with the Court of Chancery, another of the king's courts. Coke viewed Chancery as a threat to the common law. He was determined to stop the Court of Chancery from interfering with common-law courts.

The Court of Chancery had arisen in response to the common law. When the common law was developing, courts had created new writs to give people their day in court. By 1300, however, the common law had grown rigid, and injustices sometimes occurred.

When people could not find satisfaction in the common-law courts, they petitioned the king. The king referred the petitions to one of his high officials, the chancellor. He became known as the "keeper of the king's conscience." By the 1500s, a new court had arisen, the Court of Chancery, and the court's system of law was called equity. Equity was specifically developed to correct defects in the common law that caused injustices to occur. The injustices occurred in three main areas.

First, the common law had stopped creating new writs. If a person did not have an action under a writ, the person could not sue. Equity would hear these cases. It developed the following maxim, or saying: "Equity will not suffer a wrong without a remedy."

Second, the common law had settled on one main remedy—money damages. If a plaintiff sued and won in a common-law court, the plaintiff was awarded money as compensation. In some circumstances, this was not adequate. For example, if a person had a contract to buy a house and the seller backed out of the contract, the buyer could sue for money damages. The damages would be difference between the selling price and the actual value of the house. But the buyer had wanted the house. In this situation, the Court of Chancery would order the seller to perform the contract as promised. This remedy was known as "specific performance."

The most important remedy of equity was the injunction, a court order. If, for example, someone were about to do harm, the common-law courts could do nothing. The claim was not yet "ripe." The person had to wait for the harm to be done and then sue for damages. But the Court of Chancery could issue an injunction against doing the harm. Anyone violating an injunction could be jailed or fined for contempt of court.

The third area of injustice was that the common law often followed the strict letter of the law and ignored resulting injustices. Take the following example: A person borrowed money and signed a sealed document, known as a bond, promising to pay the money back. When the bond was due, he paid the creditor. If he did not get a release under seal, however, the creditor could sue him at common law to pay the debt again. And he would win. The judges at common law would defend their decision by stating everyone knew that a sealed document required a sealed release. The form mattered more than the substance. The Court of Chancery stopped this injustice. If the creditor had not yet sued, the court would order

Common Law Versus Equity

England maintained two parallel court systems for handling lawsuits—common law and equity.

	Common Law	Equity
courts	King's Bench Common Pleas Exchequer	Court of Chancery
fact finder	jury	judge
relief	damages	injunction specific performance
decisions based on . . .	the law	fairness and good faith

The three common-law courts dealt with different matters. The Court of Common Pleas was the oldest of these courts and heard lawsuits between private parties. The Court of the Exchequer heard cases related to the king's treasury. (The name exchequer comes from a table with a checkered top in the revenue office.) The Court of the King's Bench heard cases concerning the crown and criminal matters. (When the monarch was female, the court's name was the Queen's Bench.)

him to bring the bond to court, and the court would invalidate it. If the creditor had sued, it would issue an injunction ordering him not to collect on the judgment.

Unlike common-law courts, the Court of Chancery had no jury. If, for example, the buyer in a land-sale contract petitioned the court for specific performance, the Court of Chancery would issue a written subpoena to the seller. The subpoena ordered the seller to appear in court. Failure to appear resulted in a fine, and most chose to appear. In court, the judge asked the seller whether he had broken his contract to sell the land. If he admitted it, the judge would order the seller to sell the land to the buyer. If he refused, the Court of Chancery would hold him in contempt. He would be jailed or fined until he obeyed the order. If the seller claimed the buyer had broken the contract, then the court would hear evidence before making a decision on granting specific performance.

By 1600, the two parallel systems—common law and equity—were firmly in place. They were also often in conflict. A judge like Coke resented the Court of Chancery preventing the enforcement of common-law judgments. He saw equity as encroaching on the common law. Judges on the Court of Chancery defended their actions citing a maxim of equity: "Equity acts in personam." This meant that equity only ordered people not to pursue their common-law judgments against other people. It never attacked or invalidated the judgments themselves.

Some common-law lawyers considered the Court of Chancery un-English. The court did not have juries, an important element of the common law. Equity's notions of "good faith," "fair dealing," and "substance over form" came from Roman law. Indeed, the lawyers at equity were trained in both Roman and common law. The chancellors were usually high church officials, educated in Roman law.

Maxims of Equity

Equity acts in personam.

Equity will not suffer a wrong without a remedy.

One who comes into equity must come with "clean hands."

Equity regards as done that which ought to be done.

Equity looks to substance rather than form.

One who seeks equity must do equity.

Equality is equity.

Where equities are equal, the first in time shall prevail.

Where equities are equal, the law must prevail.

Equity aids the vigilant, not those who slumber on their rights.

Equity imputes an intention to fulfill an obligation.

Equity follows the law.

Equity will not concern itself with abstract wrongs.

Equity abhors a forfeiture.

Equity does not require an idle gesture.

Equity decrees only the right and just, and never that which would work injustice to the parties.

In 1616, Coke decided to crack down on individuals going to the Court of Chancery to get around decisions from common-law courts. He faced a tough rival in the chancellor, Sir Thomas Egerton. Egerton looked down on the cumbersome procedures of the common law. He once punished a lawyer who had presented too long a written pleading to the Court of Chancery. He ordered the lawyer to wear the pleading around his neck and had him paraded through all the courts in Westminster in disgrace.

To stop people from circumventing common-law judgments, Coke sought indictments in a series of cases. One case involved a trial for non-payment of a debt. The defendant had a witness who could prove he had paid the debt. On the day of the trial, however, the plaintiff lured the defense witness to a bar, got the witness drunk, and had another witness testify that the witness could not attend because he was dying. The common-law court had given the plaintiff a judgment of money damages. The defendant went to the Court of Chancery, which issued an injunction against enforcing the judgment because it had been obtained by fraud.

Coke presented the cases to a grand jury. When the grand jury refused to issue indictments, Coke stated he was going to impanel another grand jury. Egerton appealed to the king.

The attorney general advised the king that the law went against Coke. And he was right. For more than two centuries, the Court of Chancery had issued injunctions against enforcing common-law judgments based on fraud. The king sided with the Court of Chancery. Coke had lost this battle. In fact, the king was tired of Coke. Like all judges, Coke served at the pleasure of the king. This normally meant a lifetime appointment. But the king removed Coke from his position as chief justice.

For Discussion

1. What were the main differences between the common law and equity?
2. Equity developed to address three main problems with the common law. What were these problems?
3. Why were Coke and some other common-law lawyers opposed to the Court of Chancery?
4. The noted English legal historian Edward Maitland (1850–1906) once stated: "Equity saved the common law." What do you think he meant? Do you agree with him? Explain.
5. Why did James dismiss Coke from the bench? For what reasons do you think a judge should be removed from office? Why?

ACTIVITY

Equity Decisions

The Court of Chancery developed maxims of equity and used them to help decide cases. Imagine that you are a court of equity and must decide each of the cases below. For each case, apply to it a maxim of equity (use "Maxims of Equity" on page 19).

Do the following for each case:

1. Read and discuss it.
2. Find the most appropriate maxim of equity to apply to it.
3. Using the maxim, decide the case.
4. Be prepared to present to the class your decisions and your reasons for them.

Cases

1. Harry contracted to buy Sally's house from her. Two weeks after signing the contract, Sally broke the agreement and refused to go forward with the deal. Harry was not sure what to do. After mulling over his options for three years, he has sued Sally for specific performance of the contract. During this period, Sally has built a new addition to her house.

2. Pam, a rancher, owed feed-store owner Nancy $20,000. The two only knew each other from their business transactions. On her death bed, Pam wrote a will giving Nancy $20,000. She left the rest of her estate to her husband. Nancy is suing Pam's estate to collect $40,000 (her debt of $20,000 and the gift of $20,000 in the will).

3. A bank loaned Herb $50,000 when he took out a mortgage on his house. Under the terms of the mortgage, if Herb does not repay the bank in full by March 2, the bank will own the house. Herb did not have the money on March 2, but tried to repay the loan in full a month later. The bank refused to accept payment and is suing to take the house.

4. Joan was terminally ill for a year before she died. She had taken out a $100,000 life-insurance policy on her life, which she had been paying the premiums on every year for 15 years. This year the bill was lost in the mail, and she never received it. Ten days after the due date, the insurance company canceled the policy because of non-payment. Joan died the next day. Her husband, the beneficiary under the policy, is suing the insurance company for $100,000.

5. Sid agreed to let Art's Auction House sell his vintage car to the highest bidder. The contract gave no minimum price, but did allow Sid to withdraw the car from bidding any time before the auction began. When Sid saw that only a few people had showed up to the auction, he decided to withdraw from the auction. But Art assured him that if the bid was too low, a member of the auction house would place a phony bid to inflate the price. Sid decided to go ahead with the auction. His car sold for $10,000, about $50,000 less than he expected. The auction house did not place any phony bids. Sid is suing Art's Auction House for fraud.

The Case of the Five Knights

Coke had taken great risks by speaking out against the king. Many officials who were dismissed were tried for treason. But Coke managed to get back in the king's good graces within a year. By 1617, Coke had returned to the king's Privy Council. Three years later, he became a member of Parliament. The king fully expected his support. He was to be disappointed once again.

The beginning of what would be the Thirty Years War was spreading through Europe. When James asked for money, Parliament demanded that Protestant England abandon its proposed alliance with Catholic Spain. James angrily responded that Parliament had no right to give him advice on such matters. Coke led Parliament in drafting a protest petition:

> That the liberties, franchises, privileges and jurisdictions of Parliament are the ancient and undoubted birthright and inheritance of the subjects of England . . . the arduous and urgent affairs concerning the King, State, and defence of the realm . . . are proper subjects and matters of counsel and debate in Parliament . . . And that . . . every member of the House of Parliament hath, and of right ought to have, freedom of speech . . . .

James dissolved Parliament. His Privy Council called for Coke and imprisoned him in the Tower of London. James went to Parliament and asked the clerk to show him Parliament's record of the protest petition. The clerk opened the book, and James tore the page out.

Coke spent seven months in the Tower. The king's officers searched through Coke's papers for evidence of treason, but found nothing. Coke later complained:

> I was committed to the Tower, and all my books and study searched, and 37 manuscripts were taken away. Thirty-four were restored, and I would give 300 pounds for the other three.

King Charles I (1600–1649) believed in the absolute power of kings. His reign ended in civil war between his supporters and supporters of Parliament.

King James died in 1625, and his son Charles I began his troubled reign as king. Charles shared James' belief in the absolute power of kings. James' alliance with Spain had fallen through, and England had formed an alliance with France. Charles needed money from Parliament for the war, but members of Parliament, including Coke, wanted an accounting of how the money was to be spent. The king refused, and Parliament sent him little money.

The next year, the king craftily removed troublemakers such as Coke from Parliament. He appointed them sheriffs of different counties. As sheriffs, they could not leave their counties for a year. Thus they could not attend Parliament.

The war was not going well for England. Led by the Duke of Buckingham, English forces had suffered terrible defeats. The duke, a favorite of James, had earned Charles' wholehearted support.

Parliament

Parliament was divided into two houses—the House of Lords and the House of Commons. Members of the House of Commons were elected by voters in districts. The House of Lords had two types of members: lords temporal (dukes, marquesses, earls, viscounts and barons) and lords spiritual (bishops of the Church of England). The lords temporal, the nobility, inherited their seats.

Either house could initiate legislation, but both had to agree to it. The Commons could impeach officials, but the Lords served as judges on the impeachment trial. The Lords also functioned as the highest appeals court in the land.

The House of Commons wanted him removed and voted to impeach him. It put the duke in custody pending the outcome of his impeachment trial. The king reacted angrily. He had two of the most outspoken members of Parliament jailed in the Tower of London. But he released them when he could not find any evidence of treason. Before the impeachment trial wound down in the House of Lords, Charles abruptly dissolved Parliament.

Charles' action ended the impeachment trial. But Parliament had not voted on any money matters. Charles still needed funds for the war, and he started using unusual methods. One was forcing people to house and feed soldiers. Another was demanding forced loans to the treasury.

The Case

Many people, including five knights, refused to make the loans and were jailed. The five knights pursued a writ of habeas corpus in the Court of the King's Bench. A writ of habeas corpus orders officials to bring a prisoner before the court. By that writ, any person who claims to be unlawfully detained must be brought into court so that the legality of the imprisonment can be determined.

The king's lawyers argued that the reason for jailing the knights did not have to be stated. The men might be dangerous to the state. It was for the king to decide. The lawyer for the knights demanded that every Englishman had a right to hear the charge against him: The king could not keep someone in jail without charging him. The court ruled otherwise: "a prisoner committed . . . at the King's command . . . was not bailable and cause for committal need not be shown."

Although the court ruled in his favor, Charles released all those jailed for refusing to make the forced loans. Charles needed to call Parliament, and he did not want it to examine the Case of the Five Knights. The parliamentary election was a landside for those opposing Charles' absolute power. It brought back Coke, all the other sheriffs, and many new opponents of Charles.

For Discussion

1. What problems did King James and King Charles have with Parliament? How did the kings try to resolve these problems?

2. What is a writ of habeas corpus? Why do you think many call it the "great writ of liberty"?

3. What was the Case of the Five Knights about? Do you think the court made the correct decision in this case? Explain.

4. In many ways, the U.S. Congress was modeled on Parliament. What similarities and differences do you see?

The Petition of Right

Charles wanted the Parliament to impose taxes to fund the war. The Parliament wanted a guarantee of English liberties before granting the crown more money. Coke spoke against the decision in the Case of the Five Knights. He stated that the case violated the basic rule of the Magna Carta that "No freeman shall be taken or imprisoned . . . except by the lawful judgment of his peers or by the law of the land." He even cited the Bible: "For it seemeth unreasonable to send a prisoner, and not withal to signify the crimes against him." (Acts 25:27)

On another day, Coke said: "The king cannot tax any by way of loans." He referred to an act of Parliament in the reign off King Edward III (1327–1377) that banned forced loans without an act of Parliament. Coke emphasized a legal maxim: The common law limited the king's power.

Parliament discovered that the court had never entered the judgment in the Case of the Five Knights. This meant it could not be used as a precedent. The attorney general had asked the clerk to enter the judgment, but the judges refused. When Coke heard this news, he fought to keep it from being entered. He stated on the floor of Parliament:

> The draft of this judgment, should it be entered, will sting us to death. What is this but to declare upon record that any subject, committed by absolute command, may be detained in prison forever? What doth this tend to but the utter subversion of the choice liberty and right belonging to every freeborn subject of this kingdom?

The House of Commons made a resolution making four demands:

- No one could be jailed without cause.
- Everyone had a right to habeas corpus.
- Anyone brought to court on a writ of habeas corpus had to be freed or bailed.
- Only an act of Parliament could impose taxes or forced loans.

The House of Lords needed to join the resolution. It dithered, but finally responded with language saying that rights came from the grace of the king. The response even said that the king could hold a person for "matters of state" and could state the cause when it was convenient.

Coke spoke for the House of Commons in rejecting the Lords response: "When the king doth a thing 'of grace,' it implies that it is not our right. . . . Reason of state lames Magna Carta . . . . Who shall judge of convenient time?"

The king sent Commons a message. He promised to uphold the Magna Carta and to "maintain all his subjects in the just freedom of the person and safety . . . ." He said: "You shall find as much security in his Majesty's royal word and promise as in the strength of any law ye can make."

When the Commons failed to respond, the king sent another message saying he would support a bill reaffirming the Magna Carta as long as Parliament did not attempt explain what the Magna Carta meant.

Coke spoke on the floor of Commons: "The king's answer is very gracious. But what is the law of the realm? That is the question! . . . [T]he king must speak by record and in particulars—not in general. . . . Let us put up a Petition of Right!"

Such a petition would require passage in both the House of Commons and Lords and the king's approval. Coke wrote the petition. It stated the grievances in the resolution and added the problem of forcing people to take soldiers in their homes. The petition cited why these things were wrong and stated that they should never occur again.

The Commons passed the petition unanimously. The House of Lords considered the petition. The

Excerpts From the Petition of Right (1628)

To the King's Most Excellent Majesty,

. . . whereas . . . by authority of parliament holden in the five-and-twentieth year of the reign of King Edward III, it is declared and enacted, that from thenceforth no person should be compelled to make any loans to the king against his will . . . .

II. Yet nevertheless of late . . . your people have been in divers places assembled, and required to lend certain sums of money unto your Majesty, and many of them, upon their refusal so to do, . . . have been therefore imprisoned . . . against the laws and free custom of the realm.

III. And whereas also by the statute called 'The Great Charter of the Liberties of England [Magna Carta],' it is declared and enacted, that no freeman may be taken or imprisoned or be disseized of his freehold or liberties, or his free customs, or be outlawed or exiled, or in any manner destroyed, but by the lawful judgment of his peers, or by the law of the land.

IV. And in the eight-and-twentieth year of the reign of King Edward III, it was declared and enacted by authority of parliament, that no man, of what estate or condition that he be, should be put out of his land or tenements, nor taken, nor imprisoned, nor disinherited nor put to death without being brought to answer by due process of law.

V. Nevertheless, . . . your subjects have of late been imprisoned without any cause showed; and when for their deliverance they were brought before your justices by . . . writs of habeas corpus, . . . they . . . were returned back to several prisons, without being charged with anything to which they might make answer according to the law.

VI. And whereas of late great companies of soldiers and mariners have been dispersed into divers counties of the realm, and the inhabitants against their wills have been compelled to receive them into their houses . . .

. . .

X. They do therefore humbly pray your most excellent Majesty, that no man hereafter be compelled to make or yield any gift, loan, benevolence, tax, or such like charge, without common consent by act of parliament; and that none be . . . confined, or otherwise molested . . . for refusal thereof; and that no freeman, in any such manner as is before mentioned, be imprisoned or detained; and that your Majesty would be pleased to remove the said soldiers and mariners, and that your people may not be so burdened in time to come . . . .

king sent a message saying it would erode his power if he could not jail someone without stating the cause. But he promised that he would never do such a thing except for a good reason.

The Lords voted to support the petition. But they added the following words:

> We humbly present this petition to your Majesty, not only with a care for preservation of liberties, but with a due regard to leave entire that sovereign power wherewith your Majesty is intrusted for the protection, safety, and happiness of your people.

The Commons was outraged. Coke stated that:

> [*S*]*overeign power* is no Parliamentary word. Should we now add it, we shall weaken the foundation of law and then the building must . . . fall. . . . Magna Carta is such a fellow that he will have no sovereign.

The Commons got the Lords to withdraw the clause. The Lords sent the king a separate letter saying that they still obeyed their oath of office to support the king.

The king was in desperate need of funds. He came to Parliament. The Petition of Right was read aloud to him. According to tradition, he was to speak the French words, "*Soit droit fait comme il est desire* [Let right be done as is desired]." But the king only responded that he would uphold the law, which he was obliged to do in conscience and by his power.

The next couple of days, the Commons did not know what to do. Then the cry went out to impeach the Duke of Buckingham again. The Commons met in closed session, but one member went to the king. The king sent back a message for Parliament to adjourn for the day. But the two houses sent the king back a message asking for a clear response to the petition.

The next day, the king arrived at Parliament. He said he did not understand what the fuss was about. He had clearly accepted the Petition of Right. It was read once more. This time he uttered the words, "*Soit droit fait comme il est desire.*" Cheers filled the room. All of London celebrated.

That was Coke's last Parliament. He spent he remaining years writing about the law. Even in retirement, Charles saw him as a threat. Charles in 1631 ordered Coke's house searched. All his books and papers were taken. Three year later, Coke died.

* * *

King Charles did not really mean to keep his word. He called the last Parliament in 1629. He ruled without one until 1640. In 1642, the English Civil War broke out between supporters of Parliament and the king. It finally ended nine years later. Charles' army was defeated, and he was put on trial and executed. In 1659, Parliament passed the Habeas Corpus Act, restating the right of habeas corpus and setting harsh penalties for any judge who refused to grant it.

England was without a king until the restoration of Charles' son, Charles II, to the throne in 1660. His son, James II, was overthrown in the Glorious Revolution of 1688. Following the revolution, the English Bill of Rights was enacted. It made clear that the king was under the law and that Parliament was the law-making body. Only Parliament could levy taxes. The king could not have a standing army without the consent of Parliament. Anyone could petition the government without fear of punishment. Religious freedom was guaranteed to members of the Protestant faith. Freedom of speech was protected for members of Parliament. The Bill of Rights even had a clause that the U.S. Bill of Rights later borrowed: "excessive bail ought not to be required, nor excessive fines imposed, nor cruel and unusual punishments inflicted."

Several years later, Parliament passed the Settlement Act. It gave judges life terms. They served during "good behavior." A hundred years later when the U.S. Constitution was written, it incorporated this rule for federal judges.

For Discussion

1. Why did Parliament draft a Petition of Right? What did the petition demand?

2. What conflict did the two houses of Parliament have with the wording of the draft? Do you think that this conflict was over significant matters? Explain.

3. What compromises did the king propose over the demands of Parliament? Do you think Parliament should have accepted any of these compromises? Explain.

4. Between the English Civil War and the end of the 17th century, Parliament enacted several important laws advancing English freedom. What were they? Which do you believe was most important? Explain.

ACTIVITY

The Suspension of Habeas Corpus

A writ of habeas corpus is a court order for the executive to produce a prisoner in court and justify the legality of the imprisonment. Known as the great writ of liberty, it is considered one of the fundamental rights of a free society. The writ of habeas corpus was carried to America by English colonists as part of the common law. The U.S. Constitution refers to it in Article I, Section 9 (the suspension clause):

> The Privilege of the Writ of Habeas Corpus shall not be suspended, unless when in Cases of Rebellion or Invasion the public Safety may require it.

In our history, it has only been suspended twice. It was suspended in parts of the United States during the Civil War and again during Reconstruction.

In this activity, your group will look at different situations and decide whether it would be justified to suspend the writ of habeas corpus or whether the writ even protects the people involved. Do the following:

a. Read each situation below and discuss how the suspension clause might apply to it.

b. Discuss and decide on answers to the questions following each situation.

c. Be prepared to report your answers and your reasons for them to the whole class.

Situations

1. In a major metropolitan area, a controversial trial ends with a verdict that disturbs many people. A protest demonstration turns into a riot. Police cannot quell the riot, more people join the rioting, and the violence spirals out of control. Whole blocks of the city are on fire. Reports of gunfire come from all over. The National Guard is called in, but rioting continues for weeks. It might last for months. Would a suspension of habeas corpus be justified in this situation? Do you think it should be suspended in this situation? Explain your answers.

2. Monsters from outer space invade the United States. They disguise themselves as ordinary Americans, infiltrate positions of power, and take over state by state. Much of the Western United States is in their control, and they seem intent on taking over the whole United States. Would it be justified to suspend habeas corpus in all of the United States? Do you think it should be suspended? Explain your answers.

3. The war on terror continues. The United States picks up suspected terrorists and locks them up. Do you think suspected terrorists should have the right to habeas corpus? Do you think it should depend on whether the suspect is a U.S. citizen, a U.S. permanent resident, or a foreigner? Do you think it should depend on where the suspected terrorists are held—in the United States or on U.S. bases outside the United States? Do you think it should depend on where the suspects are apprehended—in the United States, on a foreign battlefield, in a foreign country? Explain your answers.

Later Developments in Common Law

During Coke's time, England had grown into a great trading nation. Its commercial law, however, was confused and inadequate. For example, common-law courts had held that a person could not contract to sell non-existent goods. That meant if a person had promised to deliver goods that he was going to manufacture, the contract was not valid.

Two great chief justices helped remedy the common law by adopting rules from Roman law. Chief Justice John Holt (1642–1710) served for more than 20 years. He believed the common law came from Roman law. In one case, he basically adopted the Roman law of bailments, the law governing people holding property for others. Chief Justice William Murray (Lord Mansfield, 1705–93) brought in much of the Roman law of commerce, corporations, partnership, shipping, agency, insurance, and quasi-contract. Murray was a great chief justice, but a friend of his, William Blackstone, achieved much greater renown.

William Blackstone wrote *Commentaries on the Laws of England*, a highly influential work explaining the common law.

William Blackstone (1723–1780)

The son of a merchant, Blackstone was shy and buried himself in books. He attended Oxford University, and while still at Oxford, he entered Middle Temple, one of the Inns of Court. In 1745, he was awarded a degree at Oxford in Roman law. The following year, he was called to the bar.

Painfully shy and awkward around people, he had great difficulty supporting himself as a lawyer. No law firm offered him a job. In seven years in private practice, he only had three cases. He supported himself by working at Oxford.

His friend William Murray, the future chief justice, was outgoing and influential. Murray recommended Blackstone for a job as professor of Roman law at Oxford. But the shy Blackstone did poorly at the job interview, and another person got the position. Murray then advised Blackstone to give a course at Oxford. He could not give it on Roman law, because the new professor was giving this course. Blackstone began lecturing on the common law.

No university in England had ever offered a course on the common law. His course filled a great need, as many students wanted to learn about England's law. He gave the course again and again, attracting many students. In 1756, Oxford received a gift to fund a position for teaching the common law. Oxford named Blackstone as the professor and set his salary at 200 pounds per year (about $32,000 in today's money). He was expected to give 60 lectures a year.

From these lectures, he developed his book, *Commentaries on the Laws of England*. Its four volumes were published between 1765 and 1769. The book became one of the best-selling law books ever and probably the most widely known. Book sales earned Blackstone at least 14,000 pounds in royalties (more than $2 million in today's money). The book was used by generations of law students, especially in America.

The reason for its success was that Blackstone had managed to organize and clarify the common law. From its thousands of cases and precedents, he distilled the basic principles of common law into readable, even elegant prose.

The four volumes totaled about 2,000 pages. They were organized as follows:

Volume 1: "Of the Rights of Persons" looked at laws about marriage, children, and corporations and explained the rights of individuals.

Volume 2: "Of the Rights of Things" examined property and contract law.

Volume 3: "Of Private Wrongs" explored the law of torts.

Volume 4: "Of Public Wrongs" analyzed the criminal law.

Blackstone explained the rights of Englishmen. By his time, many of our modern rights had developed, including many of the due-process rights absent at Raleigh's trial. Blackstone captured the reasoning behind due-process rights in his famous phrase, "Better that ten guilty persons escape than that one innocent suffer."

Although Blackstone believed in the rights of Englishmen as expressed in his time, he did not advocate further advances in liberty or equality. He ardently defended the status quo. He even wrote: "The king . . . is not only incapable of *doing* wrong, but even of *thinking* wrong . . . ."

He did, however, favor a few changes in the law. He believed that the courts of equity and common law should be merged. He was alarmed that juries were refusing to convict guilty defendants because for many crimes the punishment was hanging. Blackstone favored lowering the number of crimes punishable by death.

Two criticisms have been made of Blackstone's book. One was that he glorified the status quo. The other was that he had oversimplified the law and cut the complexity to satisfy a popular audience.

Bentham (1748–1832)

Jeremy Bentham was one of England's great philosophers. He was the founder of the school of philosophy known as utilitarianism. In short, this theory proposed that all actions (and laws) should advance the greatest happiness for the greatest number of people.

Bentham was a severe critic of Blackstone and the common law as it existed. He proposed many reforms. Two of them even Blackstone agreed with: Unify equity and common law and end harsh sentences that sent so many prisoners to the gallows.

Bentham believed pleading and procedure needed to be greatly simplified. He thought that legislation made for more rational laws, and he advocated a code, like the French had adopted in 1804. He thought the law should be easily found in one place.

Common Law Today

By the 19th century, common law and even equity had become extremely complex, time-consuming, and badly in need of reform. Charles Dickens wrote his 1853 novel *Bleak House* about a case, *Jarndyce and Jarndyce*, that had been going on for generations, yielding fees for lawyers and clerks and pain for everyone else involved. The case was in the Court of Chancery, an equity case. Dickens' portrayal helped produce popular sentiment for reforming the legal system.

The 1873 and 1875 Judicare Acts reformed English common law. The acts did away with separate courts of equity and common law. They created one court, the High Court of Justice. The court was governed by rules of common law and equity. When the rules differed, equity was favored over the common law.

The procedures of courts were simplified. These included the rules of evidence that had developed since Coke's time.

The jury system had been a hallmark of the common-law system. In the 20th century, however, England moved away from jury trials in most lawsuits. The United States has retained jury trials for both lawsuits and criminal cases. The Sixth Amendment to the U.S. Constitution requires it in criminal cases. The Seventh Amendment reads: "In suits at common law . . . the right of trial by jury shall be preserved . . . ." Thus the Constitution enshrines jury trials and the distinction between equity and common law. Today in the United States, if a person is seeking an injunction, the case will be heard by a judge. But a lawsuit may be tried in front of a jury.

For Discussion

1. What influence did Roman law have on the common law?
2. Who was William Blackstone and why was he important?
3. Blackstone wrote: "Better that ten guilty persons escape than that one innocent suffer." What does this mean? Do you agree? Explain.
4. Why do you think the law of equity became complex, time-consuming, and badly in need of reform by the 19th century?
5. What reforms were made in the common law by the 20th century? Which do you think was most important? Why?
6. Jeremy Bentham favored a code over the common law. Why did he think a code would be better? Do you agree or disagree? Why?
7. The common law traditionally favored jury trials in both civil lawsuits and criminal cases. What do you think are the pros and cons of the jury system?

Unit 2

The Enlightenment Philosophers

The Enlightenment saw the beginning of salons, meetings of thinkers, artists, and others to discuss the ideas of the day. In this painting, a group reads the French novelist Moliere, who made fun of these gatherings.

The Enlightenment

The period in Europe from about 1600 to 1800 is known as the Enlightenment. This was a time of rapid scientific development, exploration of the New World, and challenges to church and state authorities.

Enlightenment thinkers were deeply influenced by the rise of science. Scientists such as Johannes Kepler, Galileo Galilei, and Isaac Newton had observed nature to discover natural laws about astronomy and physics.

Enlightenment thinkers believed in the power of reason to solve the problems of humans. Starting in the 1600s, European philosophers began debating the question of who should govern a nation. Should kings continue to rule with absolute power, or should democratic forms of government develop?

Many Enlightenment philosophers used the concept of the "state of nature" as a starting point in their debate. What was the human condition before governments were formed? Many philosophers believed that people formed government based on a "social contract" between the ruler and the people. What was the agreement that had been made in this contract? The philosophers disagreed about the state of nature, the social contract, and what would make the best form of government.

Four of the most important of these philosophers were Thomas Hobbes, John Locke, Baron de Montesquieu, and Jean-Jacques Rousseau. They

Vocabulary

implied agreement (im PLĪD ə GRĒ mənt) n. A contract made not by words, but by the conduct of the parties.

inalienable (in Ā lē ən ə bəl) adj. Not capable of being transferred to another person; it cannot be sold, given away, or taken away.

metaphor (MET ə for) n. A figure of speech making a comparison between two unlike things. One thing is said to be the other. If the comparison uses the words "like" or "as," it is a **simile** (SIM ə lē).

natural law (NACH ər əl LO) n. A law believed to be derived from nature about society. A higher law than human-made law.

prime minister (PRĪM MIN i ster) n. The leader of the government in a parliamentary system.

representative government (rep rə SEN tə tiv GUV ern mənt) n. A republic. A form of democracy in which people elect others to speak for them in a legislative body.

salon (sə LON) n. A periodic gathering of intellectuals, artists, and others meant to amuse and stimulate conversation on important topics.

sovereign (SOV er ən) n. The highest authority in a government.

Pronunciation of Names

Galileo (gal ə LĒ ō) Galileo Galilei (1564–1642), considered one of the greatest scientists. He invented the first telescope suitable for astronomy, confirmed that the Earth rotates around the sun, and proved various laws of motion.

Hobbes (HOBZ) Thomas Hobbes (1588–1679), English philosopher and writer known for his dark view of human nature.

Kepler (KEP ler) Johannes Kepler (1571–1630), a mathematician and astronomer who proved that planets circle the Earth in elliptical, not circular, orbits.

Locke (LOK) John Locke (1632–1704), English philosopher and writer who first articulated the theory of government later found in the Declaration of Independence.

Montesquieu (MON tes kū) Charles-Louis de Secondat (1689–1755), baron de Montesquieu, French philosopher and writer best known for his essays and advocating a separation of powers in government.

Newton (NEW tən) Isaac Newton (1642–1727), the creator of calculus and the discoverer of the laws of gravity and other scientific laws.

Rousseau (rew SŌ) Jean-Jacques Rousseau (1712–1778), Swiss-born philosopher and writer known for his belief that society had corrupted humans.

Pronunciation Key: bat, **ā**te, **ar**e, d**ä**re, den, **ē**go, n**ew**, h**er**, bit, **ī**ce, **î**rritate, box, n**ō**, b**or**n, **oi**l, **ou**t, but, **ū**se, **ch**um, **sh**e, **th**in, ***th***e, **zh** sound in treasure or mirage; ə is the **uh** sound in unaccented syllables.

developed theories of government and natural law that had a profound effect on the French and American revolutions and the democratic governments that they produced.

For Discussion

1. What was the Enlightenment?
2. What questions about government did Enlightenment thinkers raise?
3. Why do you think Enlightenment thinkers focused on man in the state of nature and the social contract?

Thomas Hobbes (1588–1679)

In 1642, a civil war broke out over who would rule England—Parliament or King Charles I. After nine years, the civil war finally ended with Parliament victorious. Charles was beheaded. Shortly after the king's execution, an English philosopher, Thomas Hobbes, wrote *Leviathan*, a defense of the absolute power of kings. The title of the book referred to a leviathan, a mythological, whale-like sea monster that devoured whole ships. Hobbes likened the leviathan to government, a powerful state created to impose order.

Hobbes began *Leviathan* by describing the state of nature where all individuals were equal. Every person was free to do what he or she needed to do to survive. As a result, everyone suffered from "continued fear and danger of violent death; and the life of man [was] solitary, poor, nasty, brutish, and short."

In the state of nature, there were no laws or police to restore order. The only way out of this situation,

This is the illustration opposite the title page of Hobbes' *Leviathan*, his great political book written in 1651.

Excerpt From *Leviathan* by Thomas Hobbes

Hereby it is manifest that during the time men live without a common power to keep them all in awe, they are in that condition which is called war; and such a war as is of every man against every man. For war consisteth not in battle only, or the act of fighting, but in a tract of time, wherein the will to contend by battle is sufficiently known: and therefore the notion of time is to be considered in the nature of war, as it is in the nature of weather. For as the nature of foul weather lieth not in a shower or two of rain, but in an inclination thereto of many days together: so the nature of war consisteth not in actual fighting, but in the known disposition thereto during all the time there is no assurance to the contrary. All other time is peace.

Whatsoever therefore is consequent to a time of war, where every man is enemy to every man, the same consequent to the time wherein men live without other security than what their own strength and their own invention shall furnish them withal. In such condition there is no place for industry, because the fruit thereof is uncertain: and consequently no culture of the earth; no navigation, nor use of the commodities that may be imported by sea; no commodious building; no instruments of moving and removing such things as require much force; no knowledge of the face of the earth; no account of time; no arts; no letters; no society; and which is worst of all, continual fear, and danger of violent death; and the life of man, solitary, poor, nasty, brutish, and short.

Hobbes said, was for individuals to create a supreme power to impose peace on everyone.

Hobbes borrowed a concept from English contract law: an implied agreement. Hobbes asserted that the people agreed among themselves to "lay down" their natural rights of equality and freedom and give absolute power to a sovereign. The sovereign, created by the people, might be a person or a group. The sovereign would make and enforce the laws to secure a peaceful society, making life, liberty, and property possible. Hobbes called this agreement the "social contract."

Hobbes believed that a government headed by a king was the best form that the sovereign could take. Placing all power in the hands of a king, Hobbes argued, would mean more resolute and consistent exercise of political authority. Hobbes also maintained that the social contract was an agreement only among the people and not between them and their king. Once the people had given absolute power to the king, they had no right to revolt against him.

Hobbes warned against the church's meddling with the king's government. He feared religion could become a source of civil war. Thus he advised that the church become a department of the king's government, which would closely control all religious affairs. In any conflict between divine and royal law, Hobbes wrote, the individual should obey the king or choose death.

For Discussion

1. What did Hobbes believe was the human experience in the state of nature?
2. What was Hobbes' idea of the social contract?
3. What did Hobbes think was the best form of government? Why?
4. What problem did Hobbes believe religion posed to society? Do you agree? Explain.
5. Why do you think Hobbes placed such an emphasis on order in society? In what areas of the world today, do you think people might desire a strong, all-powerful leader to restore order?

John Locke (1632–1704)

John Locke was born shortly before the English Civil War. Locke studied science and medicine at Oxford University and became a professor there. He sided with the Protestant Parliament against the Roman Catholic King James II in the Glorious Revolution of 1688. This event reduced the power of the king and made Parliament the major authority in English government.

In 1690, Locke published his *Two Treatises of Government.* He generally agreed with Hobbes about the brutality of the state of nature, which required a social contract to assure peace. But he disagreed with Hobbes on two major points.

First, Locke argued that natural rights such as life, liberty, and property existed in the state of nature and could never be taken away or even voluntarily given up by individuals. These rights were "inalienable" (impossible to surrender). Locke also disagreed with Hobbes about the social contract. For him, it was not just an agreement among the people, but between them and the sovereign (preferably a king).

According to Locke, the natural rights of individuals limited the power of the king. The king did not hold absolute power, as Hobbes had said, but acted only to enforce and protect the natural rights of the people. If a sovereign violated these rights, the social contract was broken, and the people had the right to revolt and establish a new government. Less than 100 years after Locke wrote his *Two Treatises of Government,* Thomas Jefferson used his theory in writing the Declaration of Independence.

Although Locke spoke out for freedom of thought, speech, and religion, he believed property to be the most important natural right. He declared that owners may do whatever they want with their property as long as they do not invade the rights of others. Government, he said, was mainly necessary to promote the public good, which meant protecting property, encouraging

> **Excerpt From *Two Treatises of Government* by John Locke**
>
> If man in the state of Nature be so free as has been said, if he be absolute lord of his own person and possessions, equal to the greatest and subject to nobody, why will he part with his freedom, this empire, and subject himself to the dominion and control of any other power? To which it is obvious to answer, that though in the state of Nature he hath such a right, yet the enjoyment of it is very uncertain and constantly exposed to the invasion of others; for all being kings as much as he, every man his equal, and the greater part no strict observers of equity and justice, the enjoyment of the property he has in this state is very unsafe, very insecure. This makes him willing to quit this condition which, however free, is full of fears and continual dangers; and it is not without reason that he seeks out and is willing to join in society with others who are already united, or have a mind to unite for the mutual preservation of their lives, liberties and estates, which I call by the general name—property.

commerce, and little else. "Govern lightly," Locke said.

Locke favored a representative government such as the English Parliament, which had a hereditary House of Lords and an elected House of Commons. But he wanted representatives to be only men of property and business. Only adult male property owners, he believed, should have the right to vote. Locke was reluctant to allow the propertyless masses of people to participate in government because he believed that they were unfit.

The supreme authority of government, Locke said, should reside in the law-making legislature, like England's Parliament. The executive (prime minister) and courts would be creations of the legislature and under its authority.

For Discussion

1. What did Locke believe were the natural rights of humans? Which did he consider most important? Which do you think is most important? Why?
2. What did Locke believe was the purpose of government? If government failed to achieve this purpose, what did people have the right to do? Do you agree? Explain.
3. What type of government did Locke favor? Do you agree with him? Explain.
4. How did Locke differ from Hobbes?

ACTIVITY

Ideal Government

Hobbes had a metaphor for his ideal government. He said that government should be a leviathan, a mythological sea monster so powerful that it could devour whole ships. He believed a government needed to be incredibly powerful to impose order.

A metaphor compares two unlike things. It shows the connection between the two. The comparison is made without using the words "like" or "as." (A simile is a comparison using these words.)

In this activity, you will make two new metaphors, one for Hobbes' and another for Locke's view of the ideal government. You may make the comparison to a pair of animals, cities, songs . . . anything. Be creative. Your metaphors, however, should be descriptive of Hobbes' and Locke's views of the ideal government.

Create a chart. Make one side for Hobbes' ideal government and the other side for Locke's. Make pictures of your metaphors (draw them, use computer graphics, etc.). Explain that government should be a [fill in your metaphor] because . . . [give reasons]. On Hobbes' side, for example, you might say government should be a leviathan because . . . . (But don't use "leviathan" as Hobbes already made this comparison.)

Write a short paper explaining why you chose your metaphors and why they are appropriate.

Be prepared to present and explain your chart to the class.

Baron de Montesquieu (1689–1755)

When Charles-Louis de Secondat (baron de Montesquieu) was born, France was ruled by an absolute king, Louis XIV. Montesquieu was born into a noble family and educated in the law. He traveled extensively throughout Europe, including England, where he studied the Parliament. In 1722, he wrote a book ridiculing the reign of Louis XIV and the doctrines of the Roman Catholic Church.

Montesquieu published his greatest work, *The Spirit of Laws*, in 1748. Unlike Hobbes and Locke, Montesquieu believed that in the state of nature individuals were so fearful that they avoided violence and war. The need for food, Montesquieu said, caused the timid humans to associate with others and seek to live in a society. "As soon as man enters into a state of society," Montesquieu wrote, "he loses the sense of his weakness, equality ceases, and then commences the state of war."

Montesquieu did not describe a social contract as such. But he said that the state of war among individuals and nations led to human laws and government.

Baron de Montesquieu believed the powers of government should be divided among the legislative, executive, and judicial branches.

Excerpt From *The Spirit of Laws* by Baron de Montesquieu

The political liberty of the subject is a tranquillity of mind arising from the opinion each person has of his safety. In order to have this liberty, it is requisite the government be so constituted as one man need not be afraid of another.

When the legislative and executive powers are united in the same person, or in the same body of magistrates, there can be no liberty; because apprehensions may arise, lest the same monarch or senate should enact tyrannical laws, to execute them in a tyrannical manner.

Again, there is no liberty, if the judiciary power be not separated from the legislative and executive. Were it joined with the legislative, the life and liberty of the subject would be exposed to arbitrary control; for the judge would be then the legislator. Were it joined to the executive power, the judge might behave with violence and oppression.

There would be an end of everything, were the same man or the same body, whether of the nobles or of the people, to exercise those three powers, that of enacting laws, that of executing the public resolutions, and of trying the causes of individuals.

Montesquieu wrote that the main purpose of government is to maintain law and order, political liberty, and the property of individuals. Montesquieu opposed the absolute monarchy of his home country and favored the English system as the best model of government.

Montesquieu somewhat misinterpreted how political power was actually exercised in England. When he wrote *The Spirit of Laws*, power was concentrated pretty much in Parliament, the national legislature. Montesquieu thought he saw a separation and balancing of the powers of government in England.

Montesquieu viewed the English king as exercising executive power balanced by the law-making Parliament, which was itself divided into the House of Lords and the House of Commons, each checking the other. The executive and legislative branches were still further balanced by an independent court system.

Montesquieu concluded that the best form of government was one in which the legislative, executive, and judicial powers were separate and kept each other in check to prevent any branch from becoming too powerful. He believed that uniting these powers, as in the monarchy of Louis XIV, would lead to despotism. While Montesquieu's separation of powers theory did not accurately describe the government of England, Americans later adopted it as the foundation of the U.S. Constitution.

For Discussion

1. How did Montesquieu's view of the state of nature differ from that of Hobbes and Locke? Which, if any, do you think is more accurate?
2. What did Montesquieu believe was the best form of government? Why?

Jean-Jacques Rousseau (1712–1778)

Jean-Jacques Rousseau was born in Geneva, Switzerland, where all adult male citizens could vote for a representative government. Rousseau traveled in France and Italy, educating himself.

In 1751, he won an essay contest. He expressed the opinion that man was naturally good and was corrupted by society. His fresh view of human nature made him a celebrity in the French salons where artists, scientists, and writers gathered to discuss the latest ideas.

A few years later, he published another essay. He described savages in a state of nature as free, equal, peaceful, and happy. When people began to claim ownership of property, Rousseau argued, inequality, murder, and war resulted.

According to Rousseau, the powerful rich stole the land belonging to everyone and fooled the common people into accepting them as rulers. Rousseau concluded that the social contract was not a willing agreement, as Hobbes, Locke, and Montesquieu had believed, but a fraud against the people committed by the rich.

In 1762, Rousseau published his most important work on political theory, *The Social Contract*. His opening line is still striking today: "Man is born free, and everywhere he is in chains." Rousseau agreed with Locke that individuals should never be forced to give up their natural rights to a king.

The problem in the state of nature, Rousseau said, was to find a way to protect everyone's life, liberty, and property while each person remained free. Rousseau's solution was for people to enter into a social contract. They would give up all their rights, not to a king, but to "the whole community," all the people. He called all the people the "sovereign," a term used by Hobbes to mainly refer to a king. The people then exercised

Jean-Jacques Rousseau's most important political work was *The Social Contract*. He argued that the people were the sovereign.

their "general will" to make laws for the "public good."

Rousseau argued that the general will of the people could not be decided by elected representatives. He believed in a direct democracy in which everyone voted to express the general will and to make the laws of the land. Rousseau had in mind a democracy on a small scale, a city-state like his native Geneva.

In Rousseau's democracy, anyone who disobeyed the general will of the people "will be forced to be free." He believed that citizens must obey the laws or be forced to do so as long as they remained a resident of the state. This is a "civil state," Rousseau said, where security, justice, liberty, and property are protected and enjoyed by all.

All political power, according to Rousseau, must reside with the people, exercising their general will. There can be no separation of powers, as Montesquieu proposed. The people, meeting together, will deliberate individually on laws and then by majority vote find the general will. Rousseau's general will was later embodied in the words "We the people . . ." at the beginning of the U.S. Constitution.

Excerpt From *The Social Contract* by Jean-Jacques Rousseau

There is but one law which, from its nature, needs unanimous consent. This is the social contract; for civil association is the most voluntary of all acts. Every man being born free and his own master, no one, under any pretext whatsoever, can make any man subject without his consent. To decide that the son of a slave is born a slave is to decide that he is not born a man.

. . .

Apart from this primitive contract, the vote of the majority always binds all the rest. This follows from the contract itself. But it is asked how a man can be both free and forced to conform to wills that are not his own. How are the opponents at once free and subject to laws they have not agreed to?

I retort that the question is wrongly put. The citizen gives his consent to all the laws, including those that are passed in spite of his opposition, and even those that punish him when he dares to break any of them. The constant will of all the members of the state is the general will; by virtue of it they are citizens and free. When in the popular assembly a law is proposed, what the people are asked is not exactly whether they approve or reject the proposal, but whether it is in conformity with the general will, which is their will. Each man, in giving his vote, states his opinion on that point; and the general will is found by counting votes.

Rousseau was rather vague on the mechanics of how his democracy would work. There would be a government of sorts, entrusted with administering the general will. But it would be composed of "mere officials" who got their orders from the people.

Rousseau believed that religion divided and weakened the state. "It is impossible to live in peace with people you think are damned," he said. He favored a "civil religion" that accepted God, but concentrated on the sacredness of the social contract.

Rousseau realized that democracy as he envisioned it would be hard to maintain. He warned, "As soon as any man says of the affairs of the state, 'What does it matter to me?' the state may be given up for lost."

For Discussion

1. How did Rousseau's thinking on the state of nature differ from that of Hobbes, Locke, and Montesquieu?

2. How did Rousseau's thinking differ from the others on the social contract? Do you think there is such a thing as a social contract? Explain.

3. What was Rousseau's ideal government?

4. Of the four philosophers discussed in this unit, which two do you think differed the most? Why?

5. Which of the democratic forms of government proposed by Locke, Montesquieu, and Rousseau do you think is the best? Why?

6. Rousseau wrote in *The Social Contract*, "As soon as any man says of the affairs of the state 'What does it matter to me?' the state may be given up for lost." What do you think he meant? Do you agree? Explain.

ACTIVITY

The Philosophers Take a Stand

Your group has been assigned one of the four philosophers from this unit. In this activity, you will participate in a debate role-playing this philosopher. The debate questions are written below. Members of your role group will need to research your philosopher's position on the debate topics listed below. The article on your philosopher contains some clues, but you should find out more about your philosopher's views by using the school library and Internet. A good place to start your Internet research is at **www.crf-usa.org**. Click on Links, *Of Democrats & Dictators* Links, and Enlightenment Philosophers. You will find links to information on your philosopher.

Debate Topics

A. The best form of government is a representative democracy.

B. Only the president should have the power to declare war.

C. A good way to make laws is for all the people to directly vote on them.

D. Religion should be a part of the government.

E. The government should have the authority to confiscate a person's property for the public good.

Unit 3
The Code Napoleon

In 1789, the representatives of the third estate met at an indoor tennis court and took an oath creating the National Assembly, the French national legislature.

The French Revolution

The French Revolution began in 1789 after financial problems forced King Louis XVI to assemble the Estates General, the national legislature. This was the first time in almost 200 years that this body had met. It was made up of three groups, called "estates." The first estate represented the clergy; the second, the nobility; and the third estate represented the rest of the people of France (about 98 percent of the population). Each of the three estates met separately and had one vote in the Estates General. Traditionally, when voting on proposals, the clergy and nobility had voted the same way and thus won by a 2–1 vote.

When the Estates General met in 1789, however, the third estate demanded that all the estates meet together and vote as individuals. Since the third estate had more members than the other two estates combined, its members would control the new body.

When the king rejected this idea, the third estate declared itself the National Assembly and invited members of the other estates to join it. This was an act of rebellion. The king, however, was in a weak position. After some resistance, the king relented and recognized the National Assembly,

Vocabulary

canon law (KAN ə n LO) n. The law of the Catholic Church.

common law (KOM ə n LO) n. 1. The judge-made law in England that evolved over centuries. 2. Judge-made law as opposed to statutory law.

Consulate (KON sə lət) n. The name of the first government formed by Napoleon after he seized power in 1799. Napoleon was the first consul.

Estates General (i STĀTZ JEN ə rəl) n. The French national legislature before the revolution. It consisted of three groups, called "estates"—the clergy, the nobility; and the rest of the people of France.

feudalism (FEW dəl iz əm) n. The political and economic system used in Europe between A.D. 800 and 1400. It was a class system based on landholding and the obligations of the tenant to the lord.

guillotine (GĒ yə tēn) n. A device for beheading a person. It consists of a heavy blade that falls along tracks. It was invented during the French Revolution by the French doctor Joseph Ignace Guillotin.

inquisitorial system (in KWIZ ə tor ē əl SIS təm) n. A system of justice in which the judges play an active role. They may investigate the case and question witnesses. It is different from an **accusatorial system** in which the two parties present all the evidence and the judge serves as a referee.

legalism (LĒ gəl iz əm) n. A word or expression used exclusively in law. Legal jargon.

monarchy (MON er kē) n. A government led by a king or queen.

National Convention (NA shən l kən VEN shən) n. The new name of the National Assembly, the first government of the French Revolution.

penal (PĒ nəl) adj. Subject to punishment. A **penal code** is a list of laws defining crimes.

primogeniture (prī mō JEN ə ter) n. The right of the eldest son to inherit all the property of his parents.

public policy (PUB lək POL ə sē) n. A principle, plan, or course of action that a government adopts to address social, economic, or other problems.

secular (SEK yə lər) adj. Related to government; not related to religion.

testimony (TEST ə mō nē) n. Statements made by witnesses under oath.

Pronunciation of Names

Augeas (ə JĒ əs) The king of Elis who held his enormous herds in his Augean Stables. As one of his 12 labors, Hercules cleaned the stables in one day by making a river flow through them. (From Greek mythology.)

Cambaceres (kom bə SĀ res) Jean Jacques Regis de Cambaceres (1753–1824), a French legal scholar and supporter of the revolution who served as second consul in the Consulate.

Napoleon (nə PŌ lē ən) Napoleon Bonaparte (1769–1821), general, first consul, and emperor of France.

Portalis (por tol ĒS) Jean-Etienne-Marie Portalis (1746–1807), a lawyer and proponent of Roman law who was one of the drafters of the Code Napoleon.

Pothier (PŌ thē ā) Robert Joseph Pothier (1699–1772), a legal scholar who wrote books before the revolution reconciling Roman, customary, and canon law.

Robespierre (RŌBZ pē är) Maximilien Robespierre (1758–94), the leader of the French Revolution who oversaw the reign of terror.

Stendhal (sten DOL) Pen name of Marie Henri Beyle (1783–1842), the French novelist best known for writing *The Red and the Black*.

Toulon (tew LŌN) A city in southeastern France on the Mediterranean Sea.

Tronchet (TRŌN shā) François Denis Tronchet (1726–1806), a trial lawyer and advocate of customary law who was one of the drafters of the Code Napoleon.

Voltaire (vōl TĀR) The pen name of the French philosopher and writer François Marie Arouet (1694–1778).

Waterloo (WOT ər lew) A city in Belgium that in 1815 was the battle site of Napoleon's final defeat.

Pronunciation Key: bat, **ā**te, **ar**e, d**ä**re, den, **ē**go, n**ew**, h**er**, bit, **ī**ce, **ĭ**rritate, box, n**ō**, b**or**n, **oi**l, **ou**t, b**u**t, **ū**se, **ch**um, **sh**e, **th**in, ***th***e, **zh** sound in trea**su**re or mira**ge**; **ə** is the **uh** sound in unaccented syllables.

Declaration of the Rights of Man (1789)

The representatives of the French people, organized as a National Assembly, believing that the ignorance, neglect, or contempt of the rights of man are the sole cause of public disasters and of the corruption of governments, have decided to set forth in a solemn declaration the natural, inalienable, and sacred rights of man . . . .:

Articles:

1. Men are born and remain free and equal in rights. Social distinctions may be based only on the general good.
2. The aim of government is to preserve the natural and inalienable rights of man. These rights are liberty, property, security, and resistance to oppression.
3. The principle of sovereignty lies in the nation. No body or individual may exercise authority that does not come directly from the nation.
4. Liberty is the freedom to do anything that injures no one else; thus no limits may be placed on each man's natural rights except those that ensure other members of society the enjoyment of the same rights. These limits can only be made by law.
5. Law can only prohibit actions that are hurtful to society. Nothing may be prevented that is not forbidden by law, and no one may be forced to do anything except by law.
6. Law expresses the general will. Every citizen has a right to participate personally, or through his representative, in its creation. The law must be the same for all, whether it protects or punishes. All citizens, being equal under the law, are equally eligible to all dignities and to all public positions and occupations, according to their abilities, and without distinction except that of their virtues and talents.
7. No person shall be accused, arrested, or imprisoned except according to law. Anyone attempting, executing, or causing to be executed any arbitrary order shall be punished. But any citizen summoned or arrested under the law shall submit without delay, as resistance constitutes an offense.
8. The law shall provide only for punishments that are strictly and obviously necessary, and no one shall suffer punishment except one legally inflicted under a law passed and in effect before the commission of the offense.
9. As all persons are considered innocent until they have been found guilty, if arrest shall be deemed necessary, all force not essential to securing the prisoner shall be severely punished by law.
10. No one shall be disturbed because of his opinions, including his religious views, unless their expression disturbs the public order established by law.
11. The free communication of ideas and opinions is one of the most precious of the rights of man. Every citizen may therefore speak, write, and print with freedom, but shall be responsible for abusing this freedom as defined by law.
12. The security of the rights of man and of the citizen requires public military forces. These forces are therefore set up for the good of all and not for the personal advantage of those to whom they shall be intrusted.
13. Taxes are essential to maintain the public forces and to pay for the cost of administration. They should be equitably distributed among all the citizens in proportion to their means.
14. All citizens have a right to decide, either personally or by their representatives, as to the necessity of taxes; to know to what uses they are put; and to fix the proportion, the way of assessment and collection, and the duration of the taxes.
15. Society has the right to require of every public agent an account of his administration.
16. A society that does not obey the law or separate the powers of government has no constitution at all.
17. Since property is a sacred right, no one shall be deprived of it except where public necessity, legally determined, shall demand it and then only if the owner has been equitably compensated.

but he also mobilized his Swiss guard. (He could no longer trust the regular French army.) Rioting broke out, and citizens stormed the Bastille, a fortress and prison in Paris.

Learning of the rebellion, people across the country also rioted. When a mob broke into the king's palace outside Paris, he agreed to return to Paris under guard.

The Assembly began passing measures that dismantled the privileges of the nobility and clergy. It passed the Declaration of the Rights of Man, a statement of every citizen's rights. By 1791, it had written a new constitution setting up a constitutional monarchy. The king's absolute power was gone.

In June of that year, the king and queen tried to escape from France. This act inflamed radicals in the Assembly. Rumors circulated that the king and queen were trying to get other countries to invade France and end the revolution. The rumors seemed confirmed when the queen's brother, the ruler of Austria, threatened such an invasion.

In the midst of all the turmoil, the Assembly declared war on Austria. Neighboring Prussia sided with Austria. Later Britain, Spain, and Portugal joined the war against France.

As war descended on France, radicals took power in the National Convention (the new name of the Assembly). The Convention voted to create a people's army to defend France. It also ended the monarchy and condemned the king and queen to death.

In 1793, the Convention set up the Committee on Public Safety to administer the state. The head of the committee was Maximilien Robespierre, nicknamed the "Incorruptible." Seeking to purge France of its enemies, Robespierre brought charges against thousands of people. Many of them were quickly tried and executed on the guillotine. This reign of terror ended only after Robespierre was himself executed in 1794.

Following Robespierre's death, the radicals lost control of the government. A new constitution was enacted creating two legislative houses and an executive committee called the Directory. The new government found a general who could win the war for France, Napoleon Bonaparte.

For Discussion

1. What was the third estate? When its representatives declared themselves the National Assembly, why was this an act of rebellion?
2. What were the different governments of France following the revolution? Name something important that happened during each. Which do you think was most important? Why?

ACTIVITY

A New Declaration of Rights

In 1789, the French National Assembly wrote the Declaration of the Rights of Man. Imagine that you are writing this document today. What rights would you include? What rights are most important?

In your group, do the following:

a. Choose a recorder to write down your ideas.

b. Brainstorm ideas for rights. If you wish, you can use the Declaration of the Rights of Man to help give you ideas, but don't limit yourself to the rights in the declaration.

c. After you have brainstormed rights, select the five most important rights.

d. Be prepared to report your ideas to the class and give reasons why the rights you have chosen are important.

Napoleon

Napoleon, on the white horse, leads his officers across a stream.

As a military officer, Napoleon drove the British from Toulon in southern France. Promoted to general, he crushed an attempt to restore the monarchy and led the French army to victories in Italy and Egypt.

A military hero to the French people, he seized control of the French government in 1799. He immediately ordered the drafting of a new constitution. This document guaranteed that all adult males could vote, but it did not provide any bill of rights. "What the French people want," said Napoleon, "is equality, not liberty." The Constitution of 1799 also created a complicated form of government called the Consulate. But Napoleon, as first consul, held most of the power. Tired of revolutionary chaos and war, the French people overwhelmingly voted to approve the new constitution, which promised stability if not freedom.

Napoleon quickly set to work taking control of the country by appointing cabinet ministers, provincial governors and councils, police commissioners, mayors, and judges—all loyal to him. To his credit, Napoleon selected appointees who usually were efficient and honest.

Napoleon also established France's first public education system and financed many public-works projects including the beautification of Paris. To end a violent conflict with the Roman Catholic Church brought on by the revolution, Napoleon negotiated a pact with the pope. The church turned its lands over to the state. In return, the government paid the salaries of Catholic priests. (Most people in France were Catholics.)

In 1800, Napoleon led his army over the Alps to defeat the Austrians in Italy. A few months later, he reached an agreement with Spain to return Louisiana to France. In 1802, a vote of the people made him first consul for life. That same year, he signed peace treaties with several countries. The short period of peace that followed allowed Napoleon to complete his plans for unifying the French nation. This included writing a new code of laws to apply equally to all French citizens regardless of class.

For Discussion

1. What did Napoleon accomplish by 1802? Which of these accomplishments do you think was most valuable? Why?

2. What did Napoleon include in his plan to unify the French nation? Why do you think this would help unify the nation?

The Law in France Before the Code

Before the revolution, French law was a tangled mess. Different legal systems controlled different parts of the country. In the south of France, Roman law prevailed. In the north, the law was based on local customs. There were more than 60 versions of regional customary law and over 300 local versions. Feudal lords, owning vast estates, insisted on their own rules. In most of France, the Roman Catholic Church's canon law set rules for marriage, divorce, and even crimes such as heresy (departing from church doctrine). For more than 100 years, French kings had issued edicts and ordinances on various subjects. The kings' law courts made rulings and created case law. The French writer Voltaire complained:

> Is it not an absurd and terrible thing that what is true in one village is false in another? When you travel in this kingdom, you change legal systems as often as you change horses.

Voltaire was one of many Enlightenment thinkers who believed in reforming the law. They thought the law should rational, simple, and uniform throughout France. Many others in France called for the law to be written down. They demanded a simple code written in language that everyone could understand. Voltaire wrote: "Let all laws be clear, uniform, and precise."

In fact, the Estates General had voted on three occasions to create a code for all of France (in 1560, 1576, and 1614). In the 100-year period before the revolution, kings had responded to the demand for a code by enacting royal ordinances on crimes, commerce, sea trading, gifts, wills, and inheritance.

Legal scholars had tried to create a model code. One presented a four-volume digest of Roman law to the king. Another, Robert Joseph Pothier (1699–1772), had tried to find similarities in the tangle of laws governing France. Combining Roman, customary, and canon law, he wrote a series of books on what he thought the law should be.

Powerful interests, however, resisted changing the law. Landowning nobles, whose word was law in their domain, saw altering the law as an assault on their power. Substantial opposition also came from the *parlements* (law courts). Many judges inherited their position on the bench and were members of the nobility. The courts were notoriously corrupt, and justice often went to the highest bidder. These judges saw codification as an attack on their privileges.

The French Revolution swept away the opposition to changing the law. The revolutionary government did away with the privileges of the nobility and all vestiges of feudalism. It eliminated the old law courts. It passed more than 15,000 new laws that changed France and tried to make all citizens equal before the law.

But these laws were not the simple, rational, logical code that Enlightenment thinkers had envisioned. Members of the government called for a new code.

The revolutionary government was searching for more rational systems in all areas. It got rid of the old system of weights and measures and replaced it with the metric system—a rational, decimal-based system. The government even replaced the old calendar with a new one of 12 months of 30 days each. (At the year's end a celebration of five or six days completed the year.) The time for a rational code of laws was at hand.

The government appointed a commission led by the legal scholar Jean Jacques Regis de Cambaceres (1753–1824) to draft a code. Cambaceres was a moderate who supported the French Revolution. In 1793, he presented a draft code containing 695 articles to the Convention. The Convention rejected it as not sufficiently revolutionary. He returned the next year with a second draft. This draft contained a mere 297 articles. Again, the Convention rejected it. One member mocked it as not a code but a table of contents for a code. In 1796, Cambaceres returned with a third draft of 1,104 articles and presented it to the Directory. It was never considered. Three years later, another draftsman submitted a proposed code to the Directory. It was similarly ignored.

Although the revolutionary governments favored a simple code. They could not agree on what it should contain. It would take the influence of Napoleon, the first consul, to create a new code.

For Discussion

1. The French philosopher Voltaire wrote: "When you travel in this kingdom, you change legal systems as often as you change horses." Give examples of what he meant. What problems might this cause?
2. Before the revolution, what attempts had been made to reform French law?
3. What forces resisted the reforms?
4. After the revolution, the opposition to reform was gone. Why do you think a new code was not enacted?

Making the Code

Determined to unify France into a strong modern nation, Napoleon pushed for a single set of written laws that applied to everyone.

In August 1800, Napoleon appointed four men to draft a code that was clear, logical, and easily understood by all citizens. Surprisingly, Napoleon did not pick Cambaceres as one of the four. Napoleon had chosen Cambaceres to be second consul. Since Cambaceres had submitted to the revolutionary governments three draft codes, he seemed a natural choice to help draft the new code.

But Napoleon wanted the code to be drafted in a spirit of reconciliation between the revolution and tradition. The men he chose were all middle-aged or older. All had worked as judges or lawyers before the revolution and were known as moderates or conservatives. Two were steeped in Roman law, and the other two in customary law. But all the drafters believed in Enlightenment concepts such as natural law. They thought they were creating a law code that all men could agree on.

One of the main writers was Jean-Etienne-Marie Portalis (1746–1807). A successful lawyer and proponent of Roman law, he had supported the revolution but not its radical elements. Radicals eventually had him thrown in jail, and upon his release, he had gone into hiding until Robespierre fell from power. Portalis stated his philosophy in drafting the code: "The spirit of moderation is the true spirit of the legislator. The political as well as social good is always found between two extremes."

The other main writer was François Denis Tronchet (1726–1806). A leading trial lawyer and advocate of customary law, Tronchet had acted as the king's defense lawyer before the revolutionary court. He was the head of France's highest court.

The four-man commission was supposed to create a logically organized, coherent code stating all

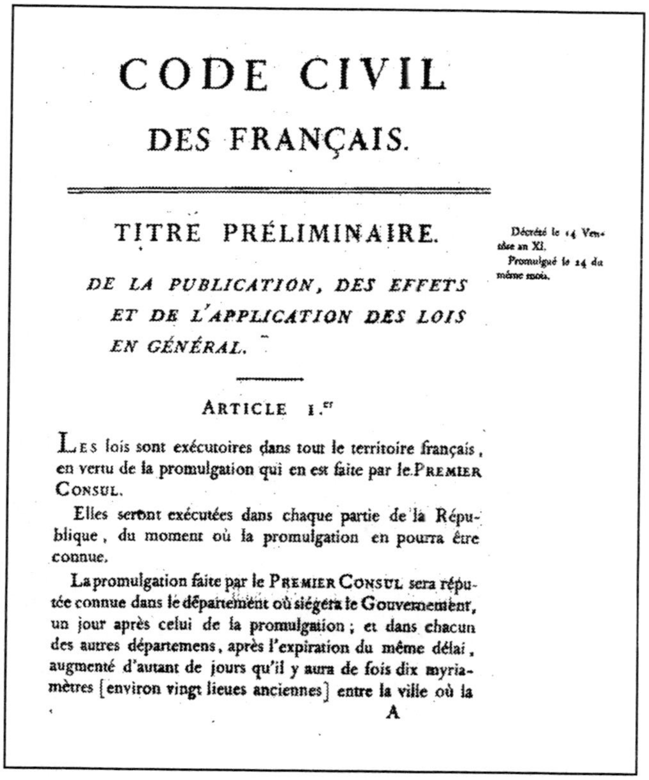

CODE CIVIL

DES FRANÇAIS.

TITRE PRÉLIMINAIRE.

DE LA PUBLICATION, DES EFFETS ET DE L'APPLICATION DES LOIS EN GÉNÉRAL.

Décrété le 14 Ventôse an XI. Promulgué le 24 du même mois.

ARTICLE 1.er

LES lois sont exécutoires dans tout le territoire français, en vertu de la promulgation qui en est faite par le PREMIER CONSUL.

Elles seront exécutées dans chaque partie de la République, du moment où la promulgation en pourra être connue.

La promulgation faite par le PREMIER CONSUL sera réputée connue dans le département où siégera le Gouvernement, un jour après celui de la promulgation; et dans chacun des autres départemens, après l'expiration du même délai, augmenté d'autant de jours qu'il y aura de fois dix myriamètres [environ vingt lieues anciennes] entre la ville où la

A

This is the first page of the 1804 edition of the Code Napoleon.

the law. Portalis did not believe the new code needed to go into great detail. He stated:

> The task of legislation is to determine the general maxims of law, taking a large view of the matter. It must establish principles rich in implications rather than go into the details of every question that might possibly arise. The application of the law belongs to the judge . . . steeped in the general spirit of the legislation. . . . There is a legislative skill as well as a judicial skill, and the two are quite distinct. The skill of the legislator is to discover the principles in each area that most contribute to the common good. The skill of the judge is to put these principles into action and to apply them to particular circumstances using wisdom and reason.

In other word, Portalis thought the code should set general principles. He thought it should be up to the courts to apply these principles to specific cases.

Napoleon agreed with Portalis. He thought highly of him, although he did think Portalis tended to drone on. Napoleon once said: "Portalis would be the most eloquent of speakers if he knew when to stop."

The four-man commission finished its first draft in only four months. It sent the draft to the highest courts for review and comments. Their suggestions were put into another draft.

The commission knew that Napoleon was going to read the draft. Napoleon was intelligent, but he was not a lawyer. The code was stripped of legalisms. It was written for the layman.

The draft of the code went to the Council of State, a group of advisors for creating legislation. Led by Napoleon, this group discussed all the provisions of the Civil Code. Many meetings began at noon and lasted through the evening and night, ending only at dawn.

Napoleon prepared for the meetings by reading law books. But he admitted: "In these discussions, I have sometimes said things that a quarter of an hour later I have found were all wrong. I have no wish to pass for being more than I really am." He listened, absorbed what was said, and often intervened to settle disputes. He was the force behind the code. He let the experts do the important work, but he helped guide the process to completion.

After the Council of State approved each section, it sent the section to the Tribunate, a legislative body that discussed pending bills. After the Tribunate discussed the bills, it sent them to the Legislative Assembly, which voted on them.

This process almost derailed the code. Two sections were sent to the Tribunate. It found them inadequate and called for the Legislative Assembly to reject them. When it did, Napoleon had to backtrack. He announced he was withdrawing the code:

> Legislators, the government has decided to withdraw the legal drafts of the Civil Code. It regretfully finds itself compelled to defer until another time the laws that the nation

awaits with interest. It is convinced that the time has not yet arrived when that calmness and unity of purpose that they require can be employed in these important discussions.

The Senate controlled the membership of the Tribunate and Legislative Assembly. Napoleon persuaded the Senate to replace those members who opposed the code. With new members, the two bodies passed the Civil Code in March 1804.

For Discussion

1. Who wrote the Civil Code? Why do you think Napoleon chose those people?
2. Why do you think the drafters did not want a detailed code?
3. The Civil Code is sometimes called the Code Napoleon. Which do you think is the better name for the code? Why?

ACTIVITY

Rational Reforms

The writing of the Civil Code was an attempt to make the legal system more rational. It encountered great resistance. Even today, resistance often greets many attempts to make systems more rational.

A. In your group, read the proposed reform assigned to your group and discuss and answer the following questions about it:
   1. What is the reform and what problem is it addressing?
   2. What are the pros of the reform?
   3. What are its cons?
   4. If proposed, would the members of your group favor or oppose this reform?
   5. Which groups or interest groups in society would oppose this reform? Which would favor it?
   6. Do you think this reform would have a chance at being enacted in today's society?

B. After discussing and answering each question, assign members of your group to report the group's answers to the class. Each group member should be assigned at least one question and should be prepared to explain the reasons for the group's answers.

Proposed Reforms

1. **The Metric System.** This is a decimal-based system of weights and measures used throughout most of the world. To measure length, the basic unit is the meter. A meter is slightly longer than a yard. A meter is divided in smaller units (e.g., decimeter [0.1 meter], centimeter [0.01 meter], and millimeter [0.001 meter]) and made part of larger units (e.g., kilometer [1000 meters]). It uses a similar decimal-based unit for volume (liter) and weight (gram).

   The metric system is far more logical than our current system of weights and measures:

   12 inches = 1 foot, 3 feet = 1 yard,
   1760 yards = 1 mile

   16 tablespoons = 1 cup, 2 cups = 1 pint,
   2 pints = 1 quart, 4 quarts = 1 gallon

   16 ounces = 1 pound, 2000 pounds = 1 ton

2. **Celsius Scale.** This is the scale used for measuring temperature throughout most of the world. Scientists and engineers in the United States also use this scale. It was created by a Swedish astronomer (Anders Celsius) in 1742, who based the scale on 0 degrees being the freezing point of water and 100 degrees the boiling point.

   The scale currently used in the United States is the Fahrenheit scale, named after German-born scientist Gabriel Daniel Fahrenheit who created the scale in 1714. It was also based on water temperature: 32 degrees is its freezing temperature and 212 degrees its boiling temperature.

3. **Dvorak Keyboard.** The current keyboard layout for most computers is called Qwerty, referring to the six letters beginning the top-left row of letters on the keyboard. This keyboard arrangement was introduced on the first typewriters to prevent the keys from jamming. With the advent of electronic typewriters and the computer, the danger of jamming no longer exists. The Dvorak keyboard was created in 1932 by August Dvorak, a professor at the University of Washington. The Dvorak keyboard puts the most frequently used keys on the home row, making typing easier and faster. According to the *Guinness Book of World Records*, the current record holder for typing speed used the Dvorak keyboard and typed 212 words per minute. Most computers provide an option for using the Dvorak keyboard, but the Qwerty layout is printed on most keyboards and taught in most schools.

4. **Simplified Spelling.** The English language is more difficult to learn how to read and write than more phonetic languages like Spanish and German. For example, a single sound such as the long *e* may be spelled using many different letter combinations: s**ee**n, sc**e**ne, l**ea**n, mach**i**ne, prot**ei**n, f**ie**ld; p**eo**ple, b**e**, k**ey**, sk**i**; debr**is**, qu**ay**.

   Proposed spelling reforms vary. Some are radical. For example, the Shavian alphabet uses non-Roman letters and has a perfect correspondence between sounds and letters. Other reforms are more modest. For example Cut Spelling keeps much of current spelling, but eliminates many silent letters in words (head = hed), vowels with schwa sounds (uh) in many words (lemon = lemn), and many double consonants (spell = spel). It replaces the letters *gh* and *ph* with an *f* when they make the *f* sound (rough = ruf and photograph = fotograf).

5. **Reformed Calendar.** The current calendar system allots the normal 365 days into 12 months of 30 and 31 days, except for the month of February, which has 28 or 29 days depending on whether it is a leap year (of 366 days). A reformed calendar would still have 12 months, but each would be 30 days long. At the end of the year, there would be five days of holidays (except in leap years when there would be six days of holidays).

6. **Esperanto.** Almost 7,000 languages are spoken in the world today. Among the most commonly spoken are Mandarin Chinese, English, Hindi, Spanish, Arabic, and Russian. Esperanto is an artificially created international language not linked to any ethnic group. It is phonetic, and its grammar is simpler and more regular than other languages. Proponents of Esperanto believe it should be adopted as the international language and taught as the second language everywhere.

7. **Plain Legal Language.** According to critics of legal writing, if a lawyer had written "Jack and Hill went up a hill to fetch a pail water," it would go something like this:

   > The party of the first part, hereinafter known as Jack, and the party of the second part, hereinafter known as Jill, did climb, ascend, or scale a hill with the purpose, intent, and goal of the aforementioned parties to bring back, carry, convey, or otherwise transport from said hill a clear, colorless, odorless, and tasteless liquid composed of two parts hydrogen and one part oxygen with a freezing point of 0° C (32° F) and a boiling point 100° C (212° F) in one [1] watertight vessel, capable of holding one [1] gallon, said vessel being cylindrical in shape, not covered at the top, and fitted with a handle.

   The plain legal language movement wants to avoid confusing legal language. It is pushing make legal contracts, jury instructions, and other legal language clearer and simpler.

The Civil Code

Enacted on March 21, 1804, the Civil Code of France marked the first major revision and reorganization of laws since the Roman era. Consisting of 2,281 short articles, or clauses, the code contained only about 120,000 words. It could be printed today as a short paperback book.

After a short preliminary section of six articles, the text consists of three parts:

Part 1. Persons. This contains 509 articles with sections on foreigners, marriage, divorce, and other aspects of family law.

Part 2. Property. It contains 185 articles on the ownership and use of property.

Part 3. How Property May Be Acquired. This is the largest part with 1,571 articles. It contains sections on contracts, torts (civil wrongs), gifts, wills, inheritance, and marriage property.

The Civil Code replaced all the old law concerning persons, property, and acquiring property. Most of the law, however, was not original. Much of it came from Pothier, a legal scholar who had tried to reconcile Roman and customary law. The rest of it came from Roman, customary, church, royal, and revolutionary law.

But it was a remarkable document. It was logical, clear, concise, and precise. Few legal terms abstractions, qualifications, or exceptions cluttered it. Written for the layman, the code explained the law so that everyone could read it and understand it.

Some considered it a literary masterpiece. The great French novelist Stendhal read a chapter daily before he began to write. He said it inspired him to write clearly and simply. The poet Paul Valery called it "the greatest book of French literature."

One reason why the code is so clear and simple is that it just covers general principles of law. Napoleon stated: "One should not burden oneself with complex laws . . . law must do nothing

The Law of Torts in the Code Napoleon

Articles 1382 to 1386, below, are the only laws on torts, or civil wrongs, mentioned in the Civil Code (1804).

1382. Every action of a person that injures another binds the person at fault to make reparations for the injury.

1383. Everyone is responsible for the damage he causes, not only by his own act, but also by his negligence or by his imprudence.

1384. A person is responsible not only for the injury caused by his own act, but also for that caused by the act of persons for whom he is bound to answer, or by things that he has had under his care.

The father, and the mother after the decease of her husband, are responsible for the injury caused by their children being minors and residing with them, for the injury caused by their servants and managers in the functions in which they have employed them; tutors and artisans for the injury caused by their pupils and apprentices while they are under their supervision.

The responsibility mentioned is incurred unless the father and mother, tutors and artisans, can prove that they were not able to prevent the act giving rise to such responsibility.

1385. The owner of an animal, or he who makes use of it while it is in his employment, is responsible for the injury that the animal causes, whether the animal were in his custody, or whether it had strayed or escaped.

1386. The owner of a building is responsible for the injury caused by its fall, when it has happened due to the lack of necessary repairs or from defects in its construction.

but impose a general principle. It is impossible to foresee every possible situation . . . ."

The entire law on torts is in five short sections. It is on the opposite page. (See "The Law of Torts in the Code Napoleon.") Its brevity contrasts sharply with the law of torts in common-law countries such as the United States. For example, the American Law Institute publishes the *Restatement of the Law of Torts*, which is a "clarification and simplification" of the American law of torts. It consists of four volumes totaling more than 2,400 pages (plus 23 volumes of appendices).

Since the Civil Code expresses only general principles, it is the job of the judge to apply them to specific situations. The code makes clear that it does indeed apply to every situation. Article 4 of the code states that "a judge who refuses to decide a case under the pretext that the law is silent, unclear, or inadequate may be prosecuted for denial of justice."

The writers of the Civil Code tried to forge a compromise between the past and the revolution. They strove for moderation. The code was an attempt to achieve national reconciliation and unification by creating uniform laws throughout France.

But it was a rational code, the product of the Enlightenment. Its purpose was not just to bring order, but also to advance many reforms started by the revolution. It had revolutionary laws in many areas, but particularly in property. It also had conservative and even reactionary laws, but many of these were similar to laws in Britain and America of that era. The most reactionary laws were those relating to women and the family.

Property Law

Like the laws enacted by French revolutionary governments, the code did away with all feudal restrictions on buying and selling property and making contracts. A contract could be made to sell anything as long as the sale did not violate public policy. (For example, selling a person as a slave would violate public policy.) Article 544 gave everyone the "right of enjoying and disposing of things in the most absolute manner, provided they are not used in a way prohibited by the laws or statutes."

The code streamlined the sale of property, even land. Roman law had required the delivery of property to complete a sale. The code did away with this requirement. Article 1583 stated that a sale "is completed between the parties, and title passes automatically to the buyer . . . at the moment when there is a meeting of the minds over the thing sold and the price to be paid for it; and this is so even if no delivery has taken place or the price has not been paid."

In one area of property law, the code turned back from the revolution. Revolutionary law had created a registry of all land. When someone wanted to buy a piece of property, he could go to the registry to see who in fact owned the land and whether any mortgages existed on the property. The code failed to continue this practice. (France started a registry system again in the 1850s.)

The inheritance of property also remained much the same as under revolutionary law. The feudal practice was known as primogeniture: The first-born son inherited all the family property. The code gave the property equally to all the children.

Before the revolution, a person was restricted from giving away property in a will. The revolution removed these restrictions. The code imposed new ones. If a person had a child, the child automatically received one-half of the property. If there were two children, they each received one-third of the property. If there were three or more children, they split three-fourths of the property. A person could only will away the property that the children did not automatically take.

Family Law

The one institution the revolution left relatively untouched was the family. The code retained many traditional rules for the family. It recognized the father as head of the household. Article 213 stated: "The husband owes protection to his wife, and the wife owes obedience to her husband." The husband managed all the family's property. A wife could make few decisions without her husband's consent. She could not sell, buy, or own property. (These laws were not changed until the 1930s.)

The old law had put many restrictions on those wanting to marry. Revolutionary laws gave any adult the right to marry. The Civil Code backtracked. A son could not marry without his parent's consent until the age of 25. Between the ages of 25 and 30, he had to formally notify his parents twice before marrying. Daughters had similar rules. They could not marry until 21, and had to notify their parents until age 25. (These laws also did not change until the 1930s.)

As for divorce, the Catholic Church had denied it. The revolution had allowed it on specific grounds or mutual agreement. The code retained divorce, but made it difficult and cumbersome. The code also removed most of the grounds for divorce leaving only adultery, long imprisonment, grievous injury, and cruelty. Napoleon insisted on adding mutual consent (Article 233). He thought it was too embarrassing to make people testify in court on these personal matters. To divorce by mutual consent, the couple had to be married more than two years and fewer than 20. Plus, mutual consent really meant the mutual consent of the family—not just the married couple. Their parents had to consent in public on four separate occasions.

Divorcing on the grounds of adultery favored the husband. He could divorce his wife if she committed a single act of adultery anywhere. A wife, however, could divorce on the grounds of adultery only if her husband had brought his mistress to live in the family home.

The father also exercised control over his children. He managed their money and decided on their education. The revolution had gotten rid of the practice of fathers being able to jail their children. The code restored it, allowing a father to jail a child for six months.

The code did, however, retain some of the changes the revolution brought to family law. The revolutionary governments had organized a system for the government to record births, marriages, divorces, and deaths. The church had previously kept these records. The code put the mayor of each city in charge of these records.

The code also did not return the authority to marry couples to the church. Secular authorities continued to perform marriages and keep all the records. After a civil ceremony, a couple could choose to have a church marriage. But the civil marriage was the official one.

Other parts of the code were quite reactionary. Article 340 banned investigating who was the father of an illegitimate child. Article 1781 ruled that an employer's testimony was to be believed over that of his employee. It also made unions and strikes illegal.

* * * * *

Between 1806 and 1810, Napoleon added a Code of Civil Procedure, Commercial Code, Code of Criminal Procedure, and Penal Code to the ground-breaking Civil Code of 1804. These codes were not as innovative as the Civil Code, and much of them was copied from previous royal codes.

The Civil Code, however, made a lasting contribution to French law. It granted individuals the freedom to contract and own property. It established equality under the law (at least for men). It banished feudal and class privileges. And it removed the church from secular matters.

The Civil Code helped lead France from a feudal society to a modern capitalistic nation. It remains in force today. Most of the original articles have not been changed. Most of the changes have been in family law.

For Discussion

1. Many have called the Civil Code a "remarkable document." What do you think they might be referring to?

2. The Civil Code contains both revolutionary and conservative (even reactionary) elements. What are examples of both in property law? In family law?

3. There are two types of codes. One type clarifies and reorganizes the law, but basically restates existing law. The other type reforms and remakes the law. Which type do you think the Civil Code is? Why?

4. French historian Albert Sorel wrote: "The *Civil Code* has remained . . . the French Revolution–organized." What did he mean by this statement? Do you agree with it? Explain.

ACTIVITY

Torts and the Code

Imagine that you are members of a French court that has several torts cases to decide. Do the following for each of the cases below:

1. Read and discuss it.
2. Read "The Law of Torts in the Code Napoleon" on page 50 and decide which article of the code applies to the case.
3. Based on the article of the code, decide the case.
4. Be prepared to report to the class your decision and your reasons for it.

Cases

1. Rosa owned a gasoline station. Each pump at the station had a large sign saying, "Do not top off." The station also had large signs saying, "No smoking." Jay was filling up his car's gas tank. When the pump stopped, he topped off his tank, but gasoline spilled on the ground and ran toward Walt, another customer. Walt had just gotten out of his car and thrown his lit cigarette on the ground. Before he could stomp it out, the cigarette ignited the gasoline, and the whole station burned to the ground. Miraculously, no one was injured. Who, if anyone, should have to pay damages to the station owner?

2. After Ken's taxi picked up Harry, Harry pulled a gun and commanded Ken to drive as he said or he would kill him. Ken drove a couple blocks, but when he made a turn, he jumped out of the taxi. Ken's taxi plowed into another car, damaging the car and injuring the driver, Suzie. Suzie is suing Ken to repair her car and to be compensated for medical bills and pain and suffering. Should Ken be held responsible?

3. At home, Mel lit candles for the holidays and left them burning. During the night, the candles fell over and started a fire. Firefighters arrived to put out the flames, and one firefighter, Jane, was injured. Jane is suing Mel. Should Mel be ordered to compensate Jane for her injuries?

4. Ned, Homer, and Lenny were hunting in the woods. Ned, who was wearing a red hunter's jacket, told the others to wait for him while he went back to the car. When he came back, Lenny and Homer had forgotten about Ned. When they heard his footsteps, they mistook him for a wild animal. They turned and fired their shotguns. One pellet struck Ned, causing serious injury. It is impossible to tell whose gun fired the pellet. Who, if anyone, should compensate Ned for his injury?

5. For several years, Tess, a powerful swimmer, had taken a daily swim across a river. One day on her swim, she noticed 10-year old Nora, a stranger to her, gasping and calling for help in the middle of the river. She decided not to save Nora because Tess had an important lunch date. Nora drowned. Nora's family is suing Tess. Should Tess be ordered to compensate the family for her death?

The Code's Legacy

In 1804, the same year that the Civil Code was enacted, Napoleon was named emperor. His armies made a string of conquests. At its height, the French empire controlled Spain, the Italian states, the German states, Denmark, and Norway.

When Napoleon decided to expand his empire into Russia, he met disaster. Russian troops kept retreating, burning and destroying everything they left behind. Napoleon entered Moscow to find the city in flames. The Russian winter was beginning, and Napoleon had to retreat with few supplies. Leaving Russian territory, the army was attacked repeatedly and suffered heavy losses from battles, frostbite, and illness. Of his 600,000 troops that invaded Russia, Napoleon returned with only 100,000.

His failure in Russia stirred Europe to rise up against him, and Napoleon suffered a string of losses in battle. The French Senate called for a restoration of the monarchy. In 1814, Napoleon was sent into exile on the island of Elba, off the coast of Italy. But early the next year, Napoleon returned to France, raised an army, and forced the new king to flee. Napoleon's return to power, however, only lasted about 100 days. In June 1815, his army was defeated at the Battle of Waterloo in Belgium. Napoleon later surrendered and was exiled to Saint Helena, an island off the west coast of Africa. He died there in 1821.

Napoleon had made his Civil Code the law in territories he conquered. Once French troops withdrew from these lands, these nations faced a choice of keeping or rejecting the Civil Code. Many nations saw the value of the code and kept it. The leaders of other countries, seeing how much their people resented Napoleon, rejected the code once the French left. But even these countries later adopted a version of it.

The Code Napoleon inspired many other nations to adopt similar law codes. Most of Europe and all of Latin America adopted versions of the Civil Code. Countries as diverse as Japan, Turkey, and Egypt have adopted it. Even some former British colonies have adopted it.

The Code Napoleon has even influenced the United States, a country steeped in the traditions of common law. In 1808, soon after President Thomas Jefferson purchased Louisiana from Napoleon, American lawmakers in the new territory wrote a code of laws largely taken from Napoleon's Civil Code. This territorial code remains as the foundation of Louisiana state law today.

The code's influence is not limited to Louisiana. Legislators in most common-law countries have created codes of law. The American Legal Institute has written model code provisions that many states have adopted.

Imprisoned on a remote island, Napoleon had many years to think about his career as a general and leader of France. He concluded: "My real glory is not the 40 battles I won—for my defeat at Waterloo will destroy the memory of those victories. . . . What nothing will destroy, what will live forever, is my Civil Code." After 200 years, the Code Napoleon continues to influence the lives of ordinary people in nearly all parts of the world. Napoleon was right. His most lasting legacy did not turn out to be his military conquests, but rather his foresight in realizing the unifying effect of a code of laws applying to all.

In 1807, the Civil Code was renamed the Code Napoleon. The official name has changed back and forth between Civil Code and Code Napoleon depending on the view toward Napoleon of those in power. The name was changed in 1816, 1852, and 1870. It currently is known as the Civil Code.

For Discussion

1. What has been the influence of the Civil Code? Why do you think it has been so widely adopted?

2. From what you know about Napoleon, do you agree that his most lasting legacy is the Civil Code? Why?

Differences Between the Civil Code and Common Law

In the Western world today, two great systems of law exist. One is based on the French Civil Code. The other is based on English common law derived from court cases. There are several basic differences between the two systems:

1. The sources of law. Both common-law and civil-code countries have constitutions and treaty obligations with other countries.

In civil-code countries, all other law comes from codes and individual statutes. There is no judge-made law. Because they are the only sources of law in most areas, codes are written in broad terms as general principles of law. The judges must apply the general rules of the code to individual cases.

Common-law countries have codes, statutes, and judge-made law. Common-law codes do not usually replace all the law in that field. These codes usually assume that common-law rules will remain unless expressly replaced in the code. The codes are not written as general principles, but in great detail with exceptions and qualifications laid out. The courts must interpret the codes, and their interpretations create case law, or judge-made law.

2. The force of precedent. In common-law countries, the force of precedent is strong. When a court decides a case, it makes law. For example, if a court interprets a statute, its interpretation forms case law. Another court deciding a similar case will look at how other courts have decided. If a higher court has ruled in this area, a lower court is usually bound to follow the higher court's decision.

In civil-code countries, precedents are not binding. A court's decision does not make case law. Judges are supposed to base their decision on the code. When the court decides a case, it simply decides that case. The decision does not affect other courts.

In France, however, there are highly regarded cases known as *jurisprudence constante.* These are lines of cases expressing the same opinion on particular issues. Many courts have accepted the reasoning in these cases. But even if a French court cites one of these cases, it still must give its own reasoning. It is not enough to cite the case. If a court is not persuaded by the reasoning in a *jurisprudence constante* case, it must follow the reasoning it considers sound. A court follows the decisions of other courts only if it finds their reasoning persuasive.

3. The way judges and lawyers reason. Because of the importance of cases and precedent, common-law courts often cite other cases. They reason by analogy: "This case is like Case A and different from Case B." Even though common-law countries have codes and statutes, their law schools teach the law by having students read and analyze cases.

In civil-code countries, the courts apply the general principles of the code to the case. The courts must base their decisions on the written law. They must look to the spirit of the code as it is thought to be a well-organized, logical whole. It is not simply a collection of laws thrown together. To aid their reasoning, courts often look at the writings of law professors on the code. Law schools in civil-code countries focus on codes and interpretations of them by law professors.

4. The use of juries. Common-law countries traditionally have used juries in both criminal cases and lawsuits. The Sixth Amendment to the U.S. Constitution guarantees criminal defendants the right to a jury trial. The Seventh Amendment guarantees the right to a jury trial in "Suits at common law . . . ." The role of the jury is to determine the facts. The judge rules on the law.

Some civil-code countries use juries in criminal cases. Most do not. None, however, uses juries for lawsuits. The court usually consists of three judges (except in some lower courts).

5. Accusatorial and inquisitorial systems. Common-law countries use an accusatorial system. The judge runs the courtroom, but does not take an active role in the case. The attorneys present all the evidence and question the witnesses. The judge acts as a referee between the two parties.

In inquisitorial systems, used in many civil-code countries, the judges play a more active role. They may investigate the case, call witnesses, and question them.

In France, a public official called the *Ministere public* is part of the judiciary. One is assigned to each case. In criminal law, the *Ministere public* acts as the prosecutor. In lawsuits, he or she represents the public.

For Discussion

1. Which of the six basic differences between the systems of law do you think is most important? Which is least important? Why?

2. If you were advising a new nation, what system of law would you advise the nation to adopt? Why?

3. Napoleon expressed dismay that people were interpreting the Civil Code: "The code had hardly appeared when it was followed almost immediately . . . by commentaries, explanations, developments, interpretations, and what not. . . . I was in the habit of saying to the Council of State: Gentlemen, we have swept out the stable of Augeas. For heaven's sake, let us not clutter it anew!" One of the first commentators was a drafter of the code. He was the first of many. If the code could fit into a small book, the commentaries would require a library. What did Napoleon mean by his statement? Why do you think the code has spawned so much commentary?

ACTIVITY

Is the Jury System Outdated?

Common-law countries have traditionally used the jury system for both civil lawsuits and criminal cases. In the 20th century, however, almost every country stopped using the jury system for lawsuits. Only two countries retain the use of juries in all civil cases—Canada and the United States. England only uses them in civil lawsuits for libel. Otherwise, lawsuits are decided by judges.

In criminal cases, about 40 of the world's 193 nations use a jury for some criminal cases. Aside from the United States, other countries that use juries in criminal cases include Ireland and many countries in the British commonwealth. Recently, Spain, a civil-code country, and Russia, a country emerging from decades of totalitarian rule, introduced juries in criminal cases.

Imagine that your group has been hired to advise a newly emerging democracy on issues of governance. You have been asked to advise whether the country should adopt the jury system for civil lawsuits, criminal cases, both, or neither.

In your group, do the following:

1. Read the pros and cons of the jury system below. These are some common arguments that can help you think up arguments of your own.
2. Discuss the pros and cons of the jury system for criminal cases.
3. Decide whether you would recommend the jury system in criminal cases.
4. Discuss the pros and cons of the jury system for civil lawsuits.
5. Decide whether you would recommend the jury system for civil lawsuits.
6. Be prepared to report your decisions and your reasons behind your decisions to the class.

Pros of the Jury System

- It keeps citizens close to the law. The law is not just in the hands of lawyers and judges.
- The jury system trains citizens in how a democratic institution works.
- It offers better decisions because the jury is a cross-section of society, not an elite that may be out of touch with many aspects of society.
- The jury can serve as a check on government power.

Cons of the Jury System

- The jurors are not experts on the law and may be swayed by emotional arguments.
- Jury members may not be well-educated and may not understand difficult matters in a courtroom, such as testimony from expert witnesses and complicated legal issues.
- It takes longer and costs more to conduct a jury trial because jury members have to be chosen, instructed in how to conduct themselves, and instructed in the law.
- Many people lose time from work to serve on a jury.

Unit 4

The Dreyfus Affair

Following his court-martial, Dreyfus went through a degrading ceremony in front of thousands of spectators. His insignia and buttons were torn from his uniform and his sword broken in half.

The Arrest and Court-Martial

In the summer of 1894, a French army officer, Major Ferdinand Walsin-Esterhazy, walked into the German embassy in Paris and offered his services as a spy. Esterhazy was deeply in debt from playing the stock market and could see no other way to raise cash quickly. Over the next few months, Esterhazy passed on French military secrets to the Germans. One of his unsigned handwritten memos told about an artillery device and a new field manual. Somehow, this memo fell into the hands of French military intelligence.

French military officials did not think the memo revealed important information. But they became alarmed that a spy, probably an artillery officer, was operating inside their own general staff. Army investigators decided to compare the handwriting on the spy document with samples of writing from suspected officers. Investigators saw a similarity in the handwriting on the memo and that of a 35-year-old officer assigned to the general staff, Captain Alfred Dreyfus.

Dreyfus made an easy target for the investigators. A stickler for military rules and regulations, Dreyfus had not gained many friends among the officer corps. More important, he was Jewish. Anti-Semitism infected much of French society. It

Vocabulary

abyss (ə BIS) n. The void; an endless hole.

acquit (ə KWIT) v. To find not guilty.

amnesty (AM nəs tē) n. A pardon to a defined group of people.

anti-Semitism (an tī SEM i tiz əm) n. Prejudice and discrimination against Jews.

coup (KEW) n. A sudden overthrow of the government done by a small group, usually military officers. Short for **coup d'etat** (KEW dā TO), which is French meaning a "blow against the state."

court-martial (KORT MAR shəl) 1. n. A military tribunal. 2. v. To try by a military tribunal.

Legion of Honor (LĒJ ən UV ON er) n. France's highest award for its citizens.

libel (LĪ bəl) 1. n. Published material that damages a person's reputation. 2. v. To publish libelous material.

pardon (PAR dən) 1. n. An official act that forgives all or part of a prisoner's sentence. 2. v. To grant a pardon.

perjure (PER jər) v. To lie under oath; to give false, misleading testimony when one has sworn to tell the truth.

perjury (PER jər ē) n. The crime of lying under oath.

Pronunciation of Names

Clemenceau (klem ən SŌ) Georges Clemenceau (1841–1929), journalist and politician. His pro-Dreyfus newspaper published Zola's open letter. He served as premier of France during World War I.

Deroulede (dā rew LED) Paul Deroulede (1846–1914), author and extreme French nationalist who tried to organize a coup against the republic.

Dreyfus (DRĪ fəs) Alfred Dreyfus (1859–1935), French army officer wrongly accused of passing military secrets to the Germans. Mathieu (MA thū) Dreyfus was Alfred's brother, who helped Alfred clear his name.

Drumont (drew MON) Edouard Drumont (1844–1917), editor of the anti-Semitic newspaper *La Libre Parole.*

Esterhazy (ES tər ho zē) Ferdinand Walsin-Esterhazy (1847–1923), a French army officer who passed military secrets to the Germans.

Zola (ZŌ lə) Emile Zola (1840–1902), French novelist and author of an open letter defending Dreyfus.

Pronunciation Key: bat, **ā**te, **are**, d**ä**re, den, **ē**go, **new**, **her**, bit, **ī**ce, **ì**rritate, box, n**ō**, **born**, **oil**, **out**, but, **ū**se, **ch**um, **sh**e, **th**in, ***th***e, **zh** sound in treas**u**re or mira**g**e; **ə** is the **uh** sound in unaccented syllables.

was particularly strong in the tradition-bound military.

The army secretly arrested and interrogated Capt. Dreyfus, but top army leaders were unsure how to proceed. They knew the case against Dreyfus was weak. Then on November 1, 1894, a Paris newspaper broke the story with the headline, "High Treason: Arrest of the Jewish Officer, A. Dreyfus." The newspaper, *La Libre Parole* ("Free Speech"), was well-known for its strong anti-Semitic views. The newspaper's editor, Edouard Drumont, stated that his information about Dreyfus had come from an anonymous source within the army. Drumont wrote that Dreyfus had made "a full confession" and that there was "absolute proof that he sold our military secrets to Germany."

These sensational revelations in the press pushed the army to prosecute Dreyfus. His court-martial and the events that followed tore France apart for 12 years. Much of the case was fought in the highly competitive French press, which created, continued, and finally brought to an end the Dreyfus Affair.

France was a deeply divided nation. Many members of the extreme right wing wanted either a strong French empire or a return to monarchy. Republicans, those favoring a democratic government, were divided between conservatives, moderates, liberals, and radicals.

The republican government had been formed in 1870 in the wake of a devastating war with Prussia. The new government consisted of a two-house legislature and a president. A previous republican government had lasted only four years from 1848 to 1852. Otherwise France had been ruled by kings and would-be emperors since 1804.

The Court-Martial

News of Dreyfus' arrest and upcoming court-martial produced a storm of newspaper stories. Newspapers bombarded the public with details of supposed evidence, unfounded charges, wholly invented events, rumors, and gossip. Leading this press frenzy were anti-Semitic journals like Drumont's paper. Drumont wrote on November 3, 1894, "What a terrible lesson, this disgraceful treason of the Jew Dreyfus!"

By the time of the court-martial in December 1894, most of the public believed Dreyfus was a traitor. The military excluded the press and public from his trial. It kept the written accusation against Dreyfus secret even from him. Despite the weak evidence, seven army-officer judges unanimously found him guilty. He was sentenced to life on Devil's Island, a prison off the coast of South America, where he would be held in solitary confinement.

Before shipping him to Devil's Island, the army put Dreyfus through a humiliating ceremony known as a "degradation." In front of assembled troops, scores of journalists, and 20,000 citizens, he was stripped of his military insignia and his sword was broken in half.

For Discussion

1. Who was Alfred Dreyfus? What was he accused of?
2. What factors led to Dreyfus' being accused?
3. How was the French nation divided politically in 1894?
4. Dreyfus' court-martial was closed to the public. What are the dangers of private trials? Do you think all trials should be open to the public? Explain.
5. What was the result of the court-martial?

A Press War Erupts

Dreyfus' family, particularly his brother, Mathieu, refused to give up. Mathieu and a helpful army officer began to turn up evidence pointing to Major Esterhazy as the real spy and traitor. In November 1897, a newspaper published a copy of the original spy memo alongside samples of Esterhazy's writing. The writing on both appeared to be identical.

As the case against Dreyfus began to unravel, the army officers responsible for his prosecution closed ranks. They believed that the credibility and honor of the entire French army were at stake. One of the officers, Colonel Hubert-Joseph Henry, had perjured himself at Dreyfus' court-martial. He now created false documents incriminating Dreyfus and leaked them to sympathetic newspapers.

Unable to ignore the mounting evidence against Major Esterhazy, the army was forced to court-martial him in January 1898. But if Esterhazy were found guilty, this would mean that important army officers either had made a terrible mistake or, even worse, had lied. Unwilling to accept these consequences, the court-martial unanimously found Esterhazy—the real spy—not guilty.

A few days after Esterhazy was acquitted, one of the country's most famous novelists, Emile Zola, published a letter to the president of France accusing high-ranking army officers of conspiring to convict an innocent man. Zola's now famous letter titled, "I Accuse. . . !" was printed in a pro-Dreyfus newspaper published by Georges Clemenceau (who would become the premier of France during World War I).

The publication of Zola's letter provoked a violent reaction. Fist fights broke out on the floor of the French national legislature. Riots occurred all over France. Mobs stoned Jewish shops and homes. Men fought duels, including one between Clemenceau and Drumont, the anti-Semitic newspaper editor (all six shots missed).

Zola was tried for criminal libel. His crime was making false accusations against the military. His letter contained many accusations, but the prosecution focused on only one: The officers at the Esterhazy court-martial knew he was guilty but were ordered to find him not guilty. Zola was to prove this was true. His attorney, Fernand Labori, tried to introduce evidence of Dreyfus' innocence. He was overruled. In fact, the judges severely limited Zola's evidence. The prosecution brought the same witnesses who testified at Esterhazy's court-martial. Many of these witnesses faltered under Labori's cross-examination. But members of the jury were intimidated by thugs demonstrating in the streets surrounding the courtroom and the publishing of their names and addresses in the right-wing press. The jury convicted Zola, but he fled to England to avoid imprisonment.

Zola's "I Accuse. . . !" also proved to be the opening shot in a bloodless press war that pitted pro- and anti-Dreyfus journalists, illustrators, and photographers against one another. The pro-Dreyfus press emphasized getting at the truth, reason, and justice for the prisoner of Devil's Island. The anti-Dreyfus journalists viewed themselves as defenders of the army and the security of the nation. Many of the anti-Dreyfus forces believed that a "Jewish syndicate," which supposedly wanted to destroy France, was behind the Dreyfus Affair.

The press war erupted when a new style of journalism was beginning to flourish in France (and in other parts of the world including the United States). New high-speed presses printed newspapers in large numbers. In Paris, nearly 100 newspapers and journals competed for readers. "Dueling newspapers" emerged specifically to attack and counterattack one another over the latest revelations in what now was simply called "The Affair."

Newly invented graphic processes allowed newspapers and other publishers to mass-produce photographs and other types of illustrations. The press war generated numerous posters, cartoons, caricatures, comic strips, picture postcards, board games, and other items that were often little more than pro- or anti-Dreyfus propaganda. One famous poster portrayed Dreyfus as a snake-like monster with a sword labeled, "The Traitor," piercing his body.

"I Accuse. . . !"

The following is an excerpt from the concluding part of Emile Zola's long letter (titled "I Accuse. . . !") to the French president. It was published in the French newspaper L'Aurore.

But this letter is long, Sir, and it is time to conclude it.

I accuse Lt. Colonel du Paty de Clam of being the diabolical creator of this miscarriage of justice . . . and of defending this sorry deed, over the last three years, by all manner of ludicrous and evil machinations.

I accuse General Mercier of complicity, at least by mental weakness, in one of the greatest inequities of the century.

I accuse General Billot of having held in his hands absolute proof of Dreyfus' innocence and covering it up . . . as a political expedient and a way for the compromised general staff to save face.

I accuse General de Boisdeffre and General Gonse of complicity in the same crime, the former, no doubt, out of religious prejudice, the latter perhaps out of that *esprit de corps* that has transformed the War Office into an unassailable holy ark.

I accuse General de Pellieux and Major Ravary of conducting a villainous inquiry, by which I mean a monstrously biased one . . . .

I accuse the three handwriting experts, Messrs. Belhomme, Varinard, and Couard, of submitting reports that were deceitful and fraudulent, unless a medical examination finds them to be suffering from a condition that impairs their eyesight and judgment.

I accuse the War Office of using the press, particularly *L'Eclair* and *L'Echo de Paris*, to conduct an abominable campaign to mislead the general public and cover up their own wrongdoing.

Finally, I accuse the first court-martial of violating the law by convicting the accused on the basis of a document that was kept secret, and I accuse the second court-martial [Esterhazy's] of covering up this illegality, on orders, thus committing the judicial crime of knowingly acquitting a guilty man.

In making these accusations I am aware that I am making myself liable to articles 30 and 31 of the law of 29/7/1881 regarding the press, which make libel a punishable offense. I expose myself to that risk voluntarily.

As for the people I am accusing, I do not know them, I have never seen them, and I bear them neither ill will nor hatred. To me they are mere entities, agents of harm to society. The action I am taking is no more than a radical measure to hasten the explosion of truth and justice.

I have but one passion: to enlighten those who have been kept in the dark, in the name of humanity which has suffered so much and is entitled to happiness. My fiery protest is simply the cry of my very soul. Let them dare, then, to bring me before a court of law and let the inquiry take place in broad daylight! I am waiting.

With my deepest respect, Sir.

Emile Zola, 13th January 1898

For Discussion

1. What caused the sensationalistic coverage of the Dreyfus case in the French press?

2. Who was Emile Zola? How did he get involved? What was he charged with?

3. Why do you think high army officials did not acknowledge their error in prosecuting Dreyfus?

4. Trials often generate sensationalistic press coverage. What examples can you think of?

ACTIVITY

Libel Law

Zola was charged and convicted of criminal libel against government officials. In most Western democracies today, criminal libel is no longer a crime.

In the United States, it is not a crime to libel government officials. But government officials can file lawsuits for libel against individuals and win money damages. These lawsuits, however, can only succeed when someone publishes something about an official with "actual malice." Actual malice in this context does not mean ill-will. It means the libelous statement was published **"with knowledge that it was false or with reckless disregard of whether it was false or not."** This rule was set forth in the 1964 case of *New York Times v. Sullivan.*

The court in *Sullivan* explained that it was not enough to allow truth as a defense to libel cases involving public officials. Proving the truth of statements can be difficult and expensive. If defendants had to prove their statements were true, many people would refrain from criticizing officials even though their criticism "is believed to be true and even though it is in fact true, because of doubt whether it can be proved in court or fear of the expense of having to do so." Requiring defendants to prove the truth of their statements "thus dampens the vigor and limits the variety of public debate. It is inconsistent with the First and Fourteenth Amendments."

Your group will role play a jury deciding libel cases. Do the following:

1. Using the rule from *New York Times v. Sullivan*, review the following cases and decide whether actual malice existed in each case.

2. Be prepared to report your decisions to the class and explain your reasons for your decisions.

Cases

1. Rumors are circulating that a city councilman is a child molester. A newspaper prints the rumors without checking them. They turn out to be false. The councilman sues the newspaper for libel.

2. A radio talk show host accuses a member of Congress of taking bribes. She admits accepting campaign contributions from certain organizations, but says they did not affect her votes. There is no evidence that these were bribes for her legislative votes. The congresswoman sues the radio host for libel.

3. A political candidate runs a campaign ad on TV that accuses the incumbent of being a "traitor" for opposing the Iraq War. The incumbent sues her challenger for libel.

4. A blogger posts an article on a presidential candidate from one of the major political parties, calling him "a paranoid religious nut." The candidate sues the blogger after losing the election.

The Unraveling of the Case

Through the summer of 1898, most of the press and the public still remained anti-Dreyfus and pro-army. But in August, one of the false documents manufactured by Colonel Henry was shown to be a forgery. Henry confessed and committed suicide. Hearing about this, the spy Esterhazy panicked and fled to England.

The case against Dreyfus was unraveling. The right-wing press, however, did not give up. One paper claimed that Henry's forgery was done to protect France from war. The army, it claimed, had conclusive evidence of Dreyfus' guilt, but to make it public would have caused a war with Germany. For this reason, it said, Henry created the forgery.

The government asked France's highest appeals court to look into Dreyfus' trial. The criminal section of the court began examining the case.

The right-wing press attacked the criminal section of the court as biased. It called for the case to be removed from the criminal section and placed before all 46 judges on the court.

Dreyfus supporters counterattacked in the press. The proceedings of the court were supposed to be private. But one of Dreyfus' lawyers got copies of the court record and sent them to *Le Figaro*, a major paper. From these leaks, the public learned how flimsy the case was against Dreyfus.

The right-wing press saw the leaks as evidence of the court's bias. It demanded the whole court hear the case. When the case was transferred to the whole court, Drumont's newspaper published the names and addresses of the judges. It asked "what precious lives are sheltered at these mysterious addresses?"

The Coup Attempt

Another threat from the right was aimed directly at the republic. When the president of the republic died unexpectedly, the two houses of the legislature elected a new man. The right believed he supported Dreyfus.

Paul Deroulede, a right-wing member of the legislature, met with his followers and plotted to overthrow the republic. On the day of the funeral, he fumed, "let us gather and . . . we will chase this newly elected man who for me is not the head of the French nation. We will overthrow this republic . . . ."

The plot, however, quickly turned to farce. The plan was to get the general in charge of the funeral parade to lead his troops against the government. After being approached, the general quietly dropped out of the ceremony. His replacement was an old general who was hard of hearing.

The new president learned of the plot and forbid the plotters from meeting. This order stopped many, but not all. On the appointed day, Deroulede grabbed the reins of the general's horse and shouted at him to follow his small group. The general could not hear what was said. He pointed his sword toward the barracks and ordered his troops to the barracks.

Deroulede was pushed back toward the barracks. Seeking to become a martyr, Deroulede demanded to be arrested for attempting to overthrow the government. Instead, he was arrested for trespassing on military property.

The Appeals Court's Decision

A Paris journalist found and interviewed Esterhazy in London. Esterhazy admitted that it was he who had written the spy memo that had started the whole Dreyfus Affair. But he claimed that he had done this on orders from his superior to prove that Dreyfus was a traitor. On June 3, 1899, the interview was published in Paris.

That same day, the court announced its unanimous decision. It voided the verdict in the first court-martial and ordered Dreyfus to be retried by the military. The court had the power to find Dreyfus innocent. But his supporters had not wanted the court to do this. They wanted

Dreyfus to be found not guilty by the military in a second court-martial.

The court's decision brought jubilation among Dreyfus' supporters and enraged his opponents. When the president of the republic visited the race track the following day, a group of right-wingers gathered around his box and chanted "Resign!" One member of the group, a baron, charged the president and swung his walking stick, knocking off the president's top hat. Two generals pounced on the man. He was arrested, convicted, and sentenced to four years in prison for the attack.

More and more of the French people sided with Dreyfus. They had read the evidence of the case in *Le Figaro*. They saw that the nation's highest court had unanimously ordered a new court-martial. They also came to see Dreyfus' opponents as opponents of the republic. The coup attempt and the attack on the president strengthened this viewpoint.

For Discussion

1. What actions did supporters of Dreyfus take to get his case reversed? What actions did opponents of Dreyfus take? Which of these actions, if any, do you consider unethical? Why?

2. What did the court decide? What impact did the decision have on France?

Dreyfus' Second Court-Martial

Two days after the court's decision, Dreyfus was handed a telegram:

> Captain Dreyfus ceases to be subject to deportation, becomes a simple suspect, is restored to his rank, and can wear his uniform. Cruiser *Sfax* departs today . . . under orders to retrieve the suspect from Devil's Island to return him to France.

Dreyfus had been in prison for four-and-a-half years—mostly in solitary confinement. He was weak, skinny, missing teeth, and unused to human company. One person described him as "a little old man—an old, old man of 39."

When he landed in France, he was reunited with his wife and brother. Joined by his lawyers, the group prepared for the second court-martial. It was to be held in Rennes, a small city in northwestern France.

This time the trial was public. In fact, Dreyfus' second court-martial was probably the world's first big media event. Hundreds of journalists, photographers, celebrities, and ordinary people from many nations wanted to witness the trial. The city's hotels were packed. The city put in additional telephone and telegraph lines to meet the increased demand. Reporters covering the proceedings tried, but were not permitted, to take motion pictures (invented a few years earlier). Soldiers patrolled the city and guarded the trial, held in a high school auditorium to accommodate the crowd.

Dreyfus had two lawyers. One was Edgar Demange, who had defended Dreyfus at his first court-martial. Conservative politically and in his courtroom style, Demange favored a defense that raised doubts about the prosecution's case.

Dreyfus' other lawyer was Fernand Labori, who had defended Zola. Known for his heated rhetoric, Labori wanted to expose the army's wrongdoing in sending an innocent man to prison. He opposed Demange's strategy of simply showing the army did not have enough proof to convict Dreyfus.

The two lawyers feuded over strategy. They showed their contrasting styles in the courtroom. Labori's fiery accusations often drew anger from the military judges. Demange was always respectful and even submissive toward the judges. By the end of the second court-martial, the two lawyers hardly spoke to one another.

No new evidence was introduced against Dreyfus. The prosecution, however, presented much evidence that had been discredited. Army witnesses testified as if the evidence were valid. Esterhazy did not return to France to testify, but sent a letter repeating his lies. Officers even testified that Dreyfus was a gambler and frequented prostitutes. Neither charge was true. When a high-ranking general said he had reviewed the evidence and would be the first to say if a mistake had been made, Dreyfus could not contain himself. He jumped up and yelled, "That is exactly what you should say!" But the general calmly concluded his testimony saying that he believed Dreyfus was guilty. The defense countered all the evidence, but the military court was predisposed to believe the army officers.

Tension was high throughout France. In Paris, opponents of Dreyfus rioted, provoking the worst street violence in the republic's short history. One week into the trial in Rennes, a man shot Labori, Dreyfus' attorney, as he walked to the court. Labori was not seriously injured, and he returned to the trial within a week.

The trial lasted six weeks. On September 9, 1899, the judges began their deliberations. An hour later, they returned with their verdict. By a 5–2 vote, the court again found Dreyfus guilty. This time he was sentenced to only 10 years in prison due to "extenuating circumstances."

Anti-Dreyfus zealots celebrated throughout the country. The reception outside France was far different. Many called for a boycott of the upcoming Exposition Universelle of 1900, a world's fair to be held in Paris.

Dreyfus spent four years on Devil's Island before returning to France to face a second court-martial.

Journalists from all over had reported on the trial. The world's newspapers condemned the verdict. The *Times* of London, for example, stated: "All the outrageous scandals which marked the course of the trial pale into insignificance beside the crowning scandal of the verdict." In New York, Governor Teddy Roosevelt reflected: "We have watched with indignation and regret the trial of Captain Dreyfus. It was less Dreyfus on trial than those who tried him."

For Discussion

1. Dreyfus' second trial was open to the public. What problems might public trials pose? What can be done to ensure a fair public trial? Do you think all trials should be held in public? Explain.

2. What was the result of the second court-martial? How was the decision different from the first court-martial? What was the impact of the decision on France?

3. What two opposing strategies did Dreyfus' lawyers pursue at the second court-martial? If you were Dreyfus, which strategy would you have wanted the lawyers to use? Why?

The End of the Affair

Amid the storm of international protest over the guilty verdict, the French government offered a pardon to Dreyfus. His supporters divided on whether he should accept the pardon, because it did not declare him innocent. But Dreyfus was in ill health and could not endure further imprisonment. He reluctantly accepted. He wrote:

> The government of the republic restores my liberty. It is nothing to me without honor. From this day forth, I shall continue to seek reparation for the terrible judicial error from which I still suffer. I wish that everyone in France should know by a final judgment that I am innocent.

The government next decided to rid itself entirely of the affair. It passed a bill granting amnesty to most of those involved in the affair. The amnesty did, however, exclude those who had plotted to overthrow the republic. Dreyfus publicly opposed the amnesty. In a letter to the legislature, he wrote:

> It benefits only scoundrels who abused the good faith of the judges; who knowingly had an innocent man condemned through lies, perjury, and forgery; and who cast me into the abyss.

The amnesty protected those who had falsely prosecuted Dreyfus. For the next half-dozen years, Dreyfus and his supporters continued to try to prove his innocence.

To get an appeal accepted, Dreyfus had to present new evidence. After combing through documents, his supporters found proof that several documents introduced at the second court-martial were forgeries.

Once again, the case was examined two times—first by the criminal section of the appeals court and then by the whole court. In 1906, the highest court in France cleared Dreyfus and reversed his convictions.

The army reinstated Dreyfus and, to make amends, made him an officer in the Legion of Honor. He received this high honor in a ceremony that took place on the same grounds where he had been disgraced nearly 12 years before.

In 1902, Dreyfus' great defender Zola had died, killed from carbon monoxide poisoning from a defective heater. Dreyfus had attended his funeral. In 1908, Zola was honored by having his ashes moved to the Pantheon, the burial place for heroes of the French nation. At the ceremony, a man fired two shots at Dreyfus, wounding him slightly. His assailant was a journalist and was acquitted at trial. Although Dreyfus had been shown innocent, the Affair still roused the passions of the French.

Dreyfus retired from the army in 1907, having risen to the rank of major. He even returned to serve his country during World War I. He died on July 11, 1935, and was buried on Bastille Day, the French patriotic holiday.

In July 2006, 100 years after the French court declared Dreyfus innocent, a ceremony was held on the grounds where Dreyfus was disgraced and later awarded the Legion of Honor. French President Jacques Chirac told the assembled crowd: "The tragedy of Captain Dreyfus continues to resonate loudly within our hearts. After dividing the country, it helped to strengthen the republic."

Guy Cavinet, the current chief justice of France's highest court, reflected on the 1906 court decision:

> The . . . court's verdict . . . continues to affirm and demonstrate the total innocence of Captain Dreyfus and his wrongful conviction on two successive occasions. The court's decision to quash his convictions stands as a sentinel to us today, we who are the direct inheritors of that legacy—magistrates, lawyers, and intellectuals who must confront political threats and maneuvers, the ignominy of odious press campaigns and the violence of crowds unleashed by nationalism and anti-Semitism.

For Discussion

1. Why do you think Dreyfus was found guilty at his two court-martials? Do you think anti-Semitism played a role? Explain your answers.

2. If you were Dreyfus, would you have accepted the pardon? Explain.

3. What arguments can you make that the press played a negative role in the Dreyfus Affair? What arguments can you make that the press played a positive role?

4. What steps, if any, could the French government have taken to ensure that Dreyfus had a fair trial? Explain your answer.

5. What similarities do you see between press coverage of the Dreyfus Affair and press coverage of crimes and trials in the United States today?

ACTIVITY

Controversial Trials in World History

Emile Zola wrote "I Accuse," attacking the injustices of the Dreyfus case. His open letter is one of the most famous newspaper opinion pieces in history.

Imagine that you attended one of the trials listed below, and you have a chance to write an opinion piece on the trial. Each of these trials was highly controversial. This is your chance to give your opinion on the trial.

Do the following:

1. Research the case at the library or on the Internet. A good place to begin your Internet research is at **www.crf-usa.org**. Click on Links, *Of Democrats & Dictators* Links, and Dreyfus Affair. You will find links to articles on your case.

2. Write your opinion of the trial. Include in your article:

   a. Enough background information so that every reader can understand what the trial was about and why it was important.

   b. Your opinion of the trial supported by reasons.

Trials

Socrates (399 B.C.)

Jesus (30 A.D.)

John (Jan) Hus (Huss) (1415)

Joan of Arc (1431)

Savonarola (1498)

Martin Luther (1521)

Thomas More (1535)

Mary Queen of Scots (1586)

Giordano Bruno (1592 &1600)

Guy Fawkes (1606)

Galileo (1633)

John Lilburne (1638 & 1653)

Charles I (1649)

William Penn and William Mead (1670)

Alice Lisle (1685)

Admiral John Byng (1757)

Louis XVI and Marie-Antoinette (1792 &1793)

Theobold Wolfe Tone (1798)

Marshal Michel Ney (1815)

Louis Riel (1885)

Oscar Wilde (1895)

Roger Casement (1916)

Mata Hari (1917)

Nelson Mandela (1963–64)

Natan Shcharansky (Sharansky) (1978)

Lindy Chamberlain (1982)

Saddam Hussein (2006)

Unit 5
The Totalitarians

Stalin acknowledges the crowd's applause in this Soviet propaganda poster. The caption says, "Beloved Stalin–the people's good fortune."

The Rise of Totalitarian States in Germany and Russia

The 20th century saw the rise of two powerful totalitarian states. In Germany, Adolf Hitler took power and set up his Nazi regime. In Russia, a revolution put a communist government in power. Led briefly by Vladimir I. Lenin and then by Joseph Stalin, the communists called their new state the Soviet Union.

World War I had helped bring both regimes into existence. The Russian Revolution broke out in 1917, a direct result of the war. Russians were being slaughtered on the German front. Calls for withdrawal from the war went unheeded by Czar Nicholas, the authoritarian and disliked monarch. His inept regime fell to revolutionaries. The first government attempted a parliamentary republic, but its leaders decided to keep Russia in the war. It was overthrown within months by revolutionaries, led by Lenin, who promised to end Russian involvement in the war and improve the economy. The communist government faced a civil war from a diverse collection of monarchists, democrats, and other anti-communists. In 1922, however, the communists won the civil war and established the Soviet Union under the leadership of Lenin. When

Vocabulary

arbitrary (AR bə trär ē) adj. Decided by chance or whim instead of from a principle or rule.

double jeopardy (DUB əl JEP er dē) n. Trying a person a second time for a crime that the person has already been acquitted of or been convicted of.

due process (DEW PRO ses) n. Fair procedures set in law.

ex post facto law (EKS POST FAC tō LO) n. A law passed criminalizing an act committed by a person before the law was passed or increasing the penalty for a crime and applying the penalty retroactively.

feudalism (FEW dəl iz əm) n. The political and economic system in Europe between A.D. 800 and 1400. It was a class system based on landholding and the obligations of the tenant to the lord.

fuehrer (FYER er) n. Hitler's title as absolute ruler of Germany. He assumed this title when President Hindenberg died in 1934 and Hitler became both head of state (president) and head of government (chancellor). (German for "leader." Also spelled **führer**.)

Gestapo (gə STOP ō) n. Short for *Geheime Staatspolizei* (German for "secret state police").

habeas corpus (HĀ bē əs KOR pəs) n. A writ, or court order, for the executive (police, prosecutors, prison officials) to produce a prisoner in court and justify the legality of the imprisonment. (Latin for "you have the body.")

Kirov (KÎR of) Sergei Kirov (1886–1934), a top Communist official during Stalin's reign whose murder was the pretext for Stalin to intensify his purges.

Nazi (NOT sē) n. The National Socialist German Workers Party. The extreme right-wing party in Germany (1919–1945) led by Adolf Hitler.

Reichstag (RĪ K shtog) n. The German parliament.

show trial (SHŌ TRĪ əl) n. Not a real trial, but one done to impress others. Its outcome is known in advance.

Social Democrats (SŌ shəl DEM ə crats) n. A German political party advocating socialism, but through gradual, peaceful, and democratic means.

SS Initials for *Schutzstaffel* (German for "protective squadron"). Originally the bodyguards of Hitler, the group became the armed units of the Nazi Party that controlled the Gestapo and the security service. Also known as the Blackshirts.

Storm Troopers (STORM TREWP erz) n. The Nazi paramilitary organization. Also known as the Brownshirts and S.A. (initials for *Sturmabteilung*).

totalitarian (tō tal ə TÄR ē ən) 1. adj. Related to a government that controls all aspects of people's lives. 2. n. A person supporting this type of government.

Pronunciation Key: bat, **ā**te, **ar**e, d**ä**re, den, **ē**go, **new**, **her**, bit, **ī**ce, **î**rritate, box, n**ō**, **born**, **oil**, **out**, but, **ū**se, **chum**, **she**, **thin**, ***th***e, **zh** sound in trea**s**ure or mira**g**e; **ə** is the **uh** sound in unaccented syllables.

Lenin died unexpectedly in 1924, Stalin became the leader of the Soviet state.

Unlike the communists in Russia, the Nazis took power in Germany years after the end of World War I. Led by Kaiser Wilhelm in the war, the defeated Germans set up a democratic government, known as the Weimar Republic. This democratic government signed the peace treaty after the war. The treaty took land away from Germany and imposed heavy reparation payments on the Germans. Many German nationalists considered the treaty a "stab in the back." Runaway inflation almost ruined the postwar economy. Before the war, 4 German marks equaled $1. By 1923, it took 4 trillion marks to equal $1. By 1924, however, inflation was under control and the German economy was recovering. Even so, the hyperinflation had caused great damage, wiping out many people's savings. Extremists of the right and left gained influence. The worldwide Depression beginning in 1929 jolted Germany. Foreign loans and investment dried up. Unemployment soared. Businesses went bankrupt.

Blaming Germany's troubles on Jews, traitors, communists, and the failures of Weimar democracy, Hitler ran for president in 1932. He lost, but earned 37 percent of the vote. Germany's troubles continued, and a year later, the president reluctantly agreed to choose Hitler as the new chancellor. Another election was called and when the Reichstag, the parliament building, mysteriously burned down, Hitler blamed the communists. He issued a new "temporary" decree, suspending constitutional rights to crush the communists. In March 1933, Hitler commanded a majority to form a new government. He submitted an Enabling Act, transferring all lawmaking powers to him and allowing him to ignore the Weimar Constitution. With the aisles packed with Nazi Storm Troopers, the parliament voted to allow Hitler to rule by issuing decrees. The Enabling Act ended democracy in Germany and made Hitler dictator.

Hitler's Germany and Stalin's Soviet Union differed in many ways. Germany was an advanced industrial nation. Russia was just emerging from feudalism. The Nazis preached an extreme right-wing ideology of nationalism, racism, and militarism. The Soviets advocated an opposing extreme left-wing ideology of communism, promising public ownership of industry and an equal share in the economy for everyone.

In practice, however, the two regimes were quite similar. They were totalitarian, meaning they controlled most aspects of people's lives. The state suppressed basic freedoms, tightly controlling religious practice, the press, and demonstrations of citizens. Individuals had to be careful of what they said or they could be arrested. Due process of law was gone. A person arrested could be tortured into confessing a "crime." Many did not stand trial at all, but were taken directly to prison camps. Those who did stand trial knew their outcome in advance. Millions perished in prison camps, many killed intentionally.

Yet the two regimes claimed to offer their people freedom. They kept the appearance of a justice system. They sometimes even held show trials of those they arrested.

For Discussion

1. What is a totalitarian regime? Give some examples from history or from the current day.
2. If World War I had never occurred, the German Nazi and Soviet Communist regimes would never have arisen. Do you agree or disagree? Explain.
3. How were Nazi Germany and the Soviet Union different? Similar?

Soviet leaders in 1929 pose for a portrait. Stalin is in the center; Kirov, on the far right. Four of the leaders died under mysterious circumstances during the purges. Many attribute their deaths to Stalin.

The Stalin Purges

Following the death of Lenin in 1924, Joseph Stalin (whose adopted name means "man of steel") had emerged as the leader of the Soviet Union. In 1929, his chief rival, Leon Trotsky, fled the country. But Stalin still wanted everyone in the Communist Party and Soviet government to bend to his will.

During the early 1930s, the Soviet economy failed. Massive food and consumer shortages plagued the Soviet people. To increase trade exports, Stalin ordered the government to confiscate all grain crops from Soviet peasants. As a result, 5 million died of starvation.

As word of the deaths and failures in the economy spread, criticism of Stalin grew within the Communist Party. In response, Stalin activated his secret police and a system of informers. Their job was to seek out and arrest "the enemies of the people who sow discord in the party." Thousands of members resigned or were expelled from the party. Many ended up banished to prison camps or deported from the country. Stalin's effort to purge the Communist Party of people who threatened his control had begun.

At the 17th Communist Party Congress in 1934, Sergei Kirov, a top party official, called for

Excerpts From the 1936 Soviet Constitution

Article 111. In all courts of the USSR, cases are heard in public unless otherwise provided for by law, and the accused is guaranteed the right to be defended by counsel.

Article 112. Judges are independent and subject only to the law.

. . .

Article 124. To ensure citizens' freedom of conscience, the church in the USSR is separated from the state, and the school from the church. Freedom of religious worship and freedom of anti-religious propaganda is recognized for all citizens.

Article 125. In conformity with the interests of the working people and to strengthen the socialist system, the citizens of the USSR are guaranteed by law:

- freedom of speech
- freedom of the press
- freedom of assembly, including the holding of mass meetings
- freedom of street processions and demonstrations.

These civil rights are ensured by placing at the disposal of the working people and their organizations printing presses, stocks of paper, public buildings, the streets, communications facilities and other material requisites for the exercise of these rights.

Article 126. In conformity with the interests of the working people and to develop the organizational initiative and political activity of the masses of the people, citizens of the USSR are ensured the right to unite in public organizations . . . .

Article 127. Citizens of the USSR are guaranteed inviolability of the person. No person may be placed under arrest except by decision of a court or with the sanction of a magistrate.

Article 128. The sanctity of the homes of citizens and privacy of correspondence are protected by law.

restraint in carrying out the purges. Later, nearly 300 of the 1,225 delegates to the congress voted against Stalin, the leader of the party. Some of the delegates even suggested that Kirov replace Stalin as party leader. Their daring to question Stalin's leadership apparently goaded him to go after the party elite.

Stalin began engineering the arrest of thousands of Communist Party and government officials. Most of those arrested were tried in secret or received no trial at all. A small minority of well-known Soviet officials did receive highly publicized public trials in Moscow between 1936 and 1938. Often based on forced confessions, the trials made a mockery of due process of law. All the participants of these "show trials," including the judges, served Stalin's political will.

Ironically, in 1936, Stalin had introduced new constitution for the Soviet Union. The constitution guaranteed Soviet citizens freedom from arbitrary arrest and the right of defense in a public trial before an independent judge "subject only to the law." The constitution was ignored.

For Discussion

1. Why did criticism of Stalin grow within the Communist Party in the early 1930s? How did Stalin respond to this criticism?

2. Who was Sergei Kirov? What threat did he pose to Stalin?

3. The Soviet constitution guaranteed its citizens due-process rights. Why do you think this constitution was ignored?

The Terror

On December 1, 1934, less than a year after he was mentioned as a possible replacement for Stalin, Kirov was assassinated. The details of the assassination still remain a mystery, but much circumstantial evidence indicates that the head of the Soviet secret police planned Kirov's murder on orders from Stalin. In any case, the assassination of an important Communist Party official gave Stalin the pretext for intensifying the purges.

Immediately after the assassination, the secret police rounded up over 100 "conspirators" and executed them. Thousands more were accused of belonging to "terrorist centers" and were shot, imprisoned, or exiled to Siberia. Still, Stalin was not satisfied. Technicians, teachers, and other government employees found themselves trapped in Stalin's dragnet. Stalin then turned on the state's security forces. Over 3,000 secret police agents were shot and one-third of the military officer corps were executed. Stalin replaced those killed with younger people loyal to him, not with the older generation of revolutionaries.

While the new Soviet Constitution of 1936 provided for due-process guarantees such as the right to defend oneself in a public trial, Stalin took steps to "simplify" the judicial system. He eliminated the right of defense. He sped up trials and often held them in secret. He suppressed the right of appeal. He expanded the death penalty to cover hundreds of offenses and extended it to children as young as age 13.

The use of terror by Stalin and his henchmen ensnared millions of Soviet citizens, most of them innocent of any wrongdoing. The terror process began with denunciations. Louis Fischer, an authority on Soviet history, explained it this way:

> Everybody played Safety First. Lying, hypocrisy . . . and disloyalty to friends were a small price to pay for keeping out of prison. To divert suspicion from yourself you accused the other fellow. . . .

Arrests usually occurred in the dead of night. Individuals were detained for weeks without any formal charges.

This statue of Sergei Kirov stands in St. Petersburg, Russia. Kirov's murder in 1934 provided Stalin the pretext for intensifying his purges.

Stalin often persecuted people not for what they did, but for who they were. Anyone having anything to do with foreigners or foreign countries automatically was suspected of spying. Suspects included entire groups of people such as foreign-language teachers, members of pen-pal organizations, even stamp collectors. Those with religious backgrounds like Catholic priests, Jehovah's Witnesses, and Jews were arrested. Agricultural officials, factory managers, and engineers were frequently accused of economic sabotage known as "wrecking." They were blamed for railway accidents, livestock diseases, crop failures, and hundreds of other shortcomings in the Soviet economy. Finally, Communist Party officials at higher and higher levels were arrested and charged with being "oppositionists" or followers of Stalin's hated rival Leon Trotsky.

The Confessions

Stalin demanded confessions from his victims. To extract these confessions, the secret police resorted to a variety of methods. The "conveyor" involved the continuous interrogation of a person by relays of police for hours and even days at a time. Intellectuals and the party elite were often subjected to the "long interrogation" by a single interrogator who carried on his questioning sometimes for weeks and months.

Some people confessed when police interrogators threatened family members. Others hoped that by cooperating they would save themselves. Many confessed under beatings and torture, at first an unofficial means of gaining a confession. In 1937, Stalin made torture the official and usual method of getting confessions. Stalin reportedly ordered the secret police to "beat, beat, and beat again."

Many caught up in the mass arrests invented "crimes" so that they could confess to something. Many admitted guilt without even knowing the charges. But some top Communist Party officials arrested on orders from Stalin confessed for quite another reason. These members of the old generation of revolutionaries came to power with Lenin in 1917 and had such faith in the party that they refused to believe it could ever be wrong. In Arthur Koestler's novel *Darkness at Noon,* the main character named Rubashov is falsely accused of plotting the assassination of "No. 1" (Stalin). Rubashov finally "confesses" after declaring, "I will do everything which may serve the Party." In the novel, he willingly took a bullet in the head after becoming convinced that he must be guilty because the party said so.

For Discussion

1. What pretext did Stalin use for intensifying the purges?
2. What methods did Stalin use to purge the party?
3. What people did he persecute? Why do you think he focused on these people?
4. Why do you think Stalin wanted confessions? Why did people confess to crimes they did not commit? How reliable do you think confessions are as evidence?

The Show Trials

Few of the thousands arrested during the Stalin purges ever saw a Soviet courtroom. Special secret police boards sentenced defendants without them even being present. "When it is a question of annihilating the enemy," Stalin's chief prosecutor pronounced, "we can do it just as well without a trial."

Between 1936 and 1938, however, Stalin conducted three show trials involving about 50 top Communist Party leaders and government officials. Stalin wanted to convince the world's press that accused criminals were being treated fairly. Also, these scripted trials were intended to discredit the old generation of Communists who still posed a potential threat to Stalin's rule.

The most serious charge leveled at the defendants was that they conspired with Trotsky (who lived in exile outside the USSR) to assassinate Lenin, Stalin, and other Soviet leaders. In addition, the accused were charged with spying for foreign powers and sabotaging the economy. The evidence consisted almost entirely of the confessions from the defendants themselves. State-appointed defense attorneys, when they were permitted, played little role in the proceedings.

The most spectacular of the show trials was the last, held in March 1938. With Stalin looking on from a darkened viewing area, the script of the trial almost fell to pieces on the first day when defendant Nikolai Krestinsky refused to plead guilty. After a night with his interrogators, he reversed himself in court the next day. "I fully and completely admit that I am guilty of all the gravest charges brought against me personally," a subdued Krestinsky said.

The most important defendant at this trial was Nikolai Bukharin, known as the "Heir of Lenin." Following the first show trial in 1936, Bukharin accused Stalin of trying to take over the Communist Party to increase his personal power. A year later, Bukharin was arrested. After interrogations that went on for more than a year, Bukharin confessed to belonging to a "Trotskyite Bloc" whose purpose was to restore capitalism to the USSR. While confessing to the general charges, Bukharin denied committing specific criminal acts such as plotting the deaths of Lenin and Stalin.

Andrei Vishinsky, the chief prosecutor, summed up the case against the 21 defendants at the last show trial. He referred to them as "a foul-smelling heap of human garbage." As for Bukharin, Vishinsky called him "the damnable cross of a fox and a swine." The chief prosecutor demanded that the accused "be shot like dirty dogs!" He concluded with this tribute to the leader of the Soviet Union:

> Over the road cleared of the last scum and filth of the past, we our people, with our beloved leader and teacher, the great Stalin, at our head will march as before onward and onward, toward Communism!

The judge found all the defendants guilty on all the charges. (There were no jury trials in the Soviet judicial system.) All were subsequently shot.

During the peak of the Stalin purges (1937–38), over 7 million Soviet citizens were arrested. Of these, more than a million were executed. Millions more died in the gulags (prison camps) of Siberia. Stalin's last major enemy, Leon Trotsky, was assassinated in Mexico in 1940. With Trotsky's death, Stalin had finally eliminated the old generation of Communists and replaced it with a new generation of party and government officials completely in the grasp of the "man of steel."

For Discussion

1. What were the charges against the defendants in the show trials? What was the evidence against them?

2. How did the show trials violate the concept of due process of law?

ACTIVITY

What Is a Forced Confession?

In 1936, Stalin put on his first show trial featuring "confessions" that we know today were the result of all sorts of intimidation and even torture. That same year, the U.S. Supreme Court held that forced confessions should be excluded from state criminal trials *(Brown v. Mississippi)*. The Supreme Court ruled that such confessions denied defendants "due process of law" under the 14th Amendment and that their use should overturn a conviction. But in a case decided in 1991 (*Arizona v. Fulminante*), the Supreme Court decided that a forced confession admitted into evidence would not automatically overturn a defendant's conviction. If enough other evidence existed for conviction, the use of a forced confession could be considered "harmless error" and the conviction could stand.

In this activity, your group must decide which of the situations described in the next column should be considered a forced confession.

As a group, do the following for each situation:

1. Read and discuss it.
2. Decide whether it is a forced confession.
3. Be prepared to report your decision and your reasons for it to the whole class.

Your group should also take a position on this question: Should any forced confession ever be admitted into court? Why or why not?

Situations

1. A confession following police beatings or other forms of physical force.
2. A confession following a threat by police to use physical force.
3. A confession following 24 hours of uninterrupted police interrogation.
4. A confession following several days during which the accused person is deprived of water, food, and sleep.
5. A confession following police interrogation of a suspect who is not permitted to speak to a lawyer.
6. A confession resulting from physical threats made by a suspect's cellmate who is actually a police undercover officer.
7. A confession made to police after they lie to a suspect about non-existent eyewitnesses.

Hitler's Rise to Total Power

The German Weimar Republic, created after World War I, failed to survive the chaos of the Great Depression of the 1930s. The elections of 1932 gave the Nazi Party many seats in the Reichstag, the German parliament. In January 1933, the German president reluctantly named Hitler chancellor of Germany. Although the Nazi Party had more seats than any other party, it did not command a majority in the Reichstag. Calling for new Reichstag elections in March, Hitler persuaded the elderly president, who was sick and feeble, to disband parliament. With the Reichstag dissolved, Hitler had the power to make emergency decrees if necessary.

On the night of February 27, 1933, the Reichstag building caught on fire. As fire fighters battled the flames, police and Nazi officials caught a man at the scene, Marinus van der Lubbe. He was an unemployed, mentally disturbed Dutch Communist.

In February 1933, the Reichstag building burned down. Hitler blamed the Communists, proclaimed a state of emergency, and did away with all civil liberties.

Hitler blamed the Communist Party for starting the fire. The Communists, Hitler proclaimed, had begun their attack on the state. He declared a state of emergency and issued an emergency decree, the Decree for the Protection of the People and the State (known as the Reichstag Fire Decree). The president signed the decree into law. This emergency decree did away with all civil liberties under the German constitution. It got rid of the freedoms of speech, assembly, and the press. It eliminated protections against unlawful searches, seizures, arrests, and detentions. The decree suspended all these civil liberties "until further notice." The emergency decree was never lifted. It stayed in effect throughout the Nazi reign.

In the middle of the election campaign, the Nazis began a campaign of terror. They arrested their political opponents, shut down newspapers and radio stations, broke up rallies and demonstrations, and burned campaign literature. Thousands went to jail. When the jails overflowed, new places were found to hold the prisoners—empty buildings, army barracks, and newly constructed concentration camps. Those in custody endured brutality and torture. Many were murdered.

The March election gave the Nazi Party and its allies a small majority in the Reichstag. They held 340 of the 647 seats. When parliament met at an opera house in Berlin, Nazi Storm Troopers surrounded the building and lined the aisles. Intimidated, members of the Reichstag voted 441 to 94 to pass the Enabling Act, giving Hitler the right to rule by issuing decrees. This law ended democracy in Germany.

The Enabling Act had required a two-thirds majority to pass. But only members of the Social Democratic Party had dared to vote against it. Members of the Communist Party were in jail. The members of other parties deluded themselves into thinking that by siding with Hitler, he would work with them.

The Communist Party had been outlawed in March. In June, the Social Democratic Party was

Excerpts From the Reichstag Fire Decree

February 28, 1933

On the basis of Article 48 paragraph 2 of the Constitution of the German Reich, the following is ordered in defense against Communist acts of violence that endanger the state:

Section 1. Articles 114, 115, 117, 118, 123, 124 and 153 of the Constitution of the German Reich are suspended until further notice. The following are therefore permitted: limits on personal freedom, freedom of opinion, including the freedom of the press, the freedom to organize and assemble, the privacy of postal, telegraphic and telephonic communications, and warrants for house searches, orders for confiscations of property as well as restrictions on property beyond the legal limits otherwise prescribed.

. . .

Section 5. The following crimes currently punished by life imprisonment are now to be punished by death: high treason, poisoning, arson, causing explosions, causing floods, damaging railways. . . .

Section 6. This decree goes into force immediately.

made illegal. The next month, all other parties were outlawed. The Nazi Party was the only legal party.

The Nazis continued terrorizing their opponents. By the end of the year, concentration camps housed an estimated 150,000 political prisoners. The Nazis held new elections in November 1933. Ninety-two percent voted for the Nazi Party. In the two other elections held while the Nazis were in power, the party received 99 percent of the vote.

For Discussion

1. What was the Reichstag fire? What effect did it have on Germany? Who do you think probably set it? Why?
2. What was the Enabling Act? How did Hitler get this passed? What was its effect?

Reichstag Fire Trial

In his rise to total power, Hitler had claimed a state of emergency existed. He repeatedly cited the Reichstag fire as proof that the Communist Party was actively engaged in a plot to overthrow the government.

In addition to the hapless Lubbe, the Nazis had arrested others as part of the plot to burn down the Reichstag building. They charged Ernst Torgler, the chairman of the German Communist Party, and three Bulgarian Communists with plotting the arson. The most important of the Bulgarians was Georgi Dimitrov, who had led a Communist uprising in Bulgaria.

Hitler wanted the suspects executed. Under German law, however, the crime of arson did not carry the death penalty. Hitler changed this by passing a new law permitting the death penalty for crimes committed between January 1 and February 28, 1933. This was an ex post facto law.

An ex post facto law applies retroactively. It makes something a crime that was not a crime when it was committed. Or, as in this case, it increases the penalty of a crime and applies the penalty to those who committed it before the new penalty was enacted. Ex post facto laws violate basic fairness. Most modern nations forbid their use. The U.S. Constitution, for example, bans ex post facto laws.

The Nazis were unsure exactly what to do about the suspects. Hitler wanted them shot without a trial. The Ministry of Justice wanted a court trial. When the ministry agreed to accept the ex post facto law, Hitler agreed to a trial.

The judge handling the investigation was told not to look into any links that the Nazis may have had to the fire. The defendants were kept in jail in chains before the trial. The court appointed lawyers for them.

The trial began on September 21 and lasted three months. Many testified. Eyewitnesses told of seeing the Reichstag building burn down. Fire experts explained how fires had been set in

Among the defendants at the Reichstag fire trial was Georgi Dimitrov, a leader of the Bulgarian Communist Party.

several places in the building. Police recounted how they had caught Lubbe at the Reichstag building. Attempting to spread the blame to the other defendants, high Nazi officials testified to the treachery of Communists.

One of the trial's highlights was the testimony of Hermann Goering, the head of the Gestapo, the state secret police. Dimitrov, one of the Bulgarian defendants, had fired his lawyer and was defending himself. In his cross-examination of Goering, Dimitrov asked whether the investigators were ordered to focus on Communists and not on the Nazi Party. The question outraged Goering. He erupted: "For me it was a political crime, and I was also convinced that the criminals had to be looked for in your party. Your party is a party of criminals that must be destroyed! And if the hearing of the court has been influenced in this sense, it has set out on the right track."

As questioning continued, Goering got even more angry. He exploded: "In my eyes, you are a scoundrel who should be hanged." Dimitrov remained calm throughout, but as Goering seethed, the judge warned Dimitrov "not to make Communist propaganda here." After more questioning, Goering threatened Dimitrov: "I shall teach you how to behave—just come out of the courtroom!" The judge did not admonish Goering for making a threat. Instead, he banned Dimitrov from the courtroom for three days.

Although the trial was rigged against the defendants, no evidence linked anyone other than Lubbe to the fire. The prosecutors moved that the charges be dismissed against the Bulgarians, but insisted that Torgler and Lubbe be found guilty.

On December 23, the court returned its verdict. It found Lubbe guilty, but no one else. All the Communists had been acquitted. The judges, however, issued a statement blaming the Communist Party for the fire: "The crime can only be the work of radical left-wing elements, who hoped to exploit it for the purpose of overthrowing the government and the constitution and seizing power. . . ."

The trial had taken place under the gaze of international publicity. In one of Nazi Germany's last acts of judicial independence, the court refused to convict the other defendants without evidence against them. It did not, however, reject sentencing Lubbe to death under an ex post facto law. He was executed on January 10, 1934.

Most historians today believe that Lubbe had something to do with the fire. They debate whether he acted alone or whether the Nazis planned the fire. They do not think the Communists had anything to do with the fire. Whether or not the Nazis actually planned the fire, Hitler used it as a pretext for seizing absolute power.

For Discussion

1. What is an ex post facto law? Do you think such a law could ever be justified? Explain.
2. What do you think Hitler wanted to achieve from the trial? Why do you think the trial turned out as it did?
3. Do you think the defendants received a fair trial? Explain.

Nazi "Justice"

Like the Soviet Union, Nazi Germany was a police state. Nazis expressed a general contempt for law, its processes, and lawyers. They thought the legal process was too slow, inefficient, and lenient. Hitler considered lawyers "parasites" and "criminals." The Nazis never bothered to write a new national constitution. They never even wrote a new code of laws. Hitler simply ruled by decree and let his secret police, the Gestapo, conduct a campaign of terror on "enemies of the state."

These enemies included political opponents—Communists, Social Democrats, and others who opposed Nazi rule. Enemies also included ethnic and religious groups—Jews, Jehovah's Witnesses, gypsies, and others the Nazis considered "impure" or non-German. Enemies of the state also encompassed homosexuals, habitual criminals, and others the Nazis believed immoral.

By the end of 1933, the Nazi state held 150,000 political prisoners in concentration camps. Most had never seen a courtroom or a judge. They were picked up by the Gestapo and jailed without trials. People simply disappeared into the camps. The basic protection of habeas corpus did not exist. In other words, no court had the power to order the Gestapo to produce a prisoner and show the reason the person was being held.

Yet the Nazi state did have laws and a judicial system. Of the 150,000 political prisoners in 1933, about 9,000 had been convicted of political crimes in courts. The Nazi judicial system perverted, often quite openly, the most basic principles of criminal justice.

Criminal Laws

One fundamental principle is that crimes and punishments must be clearly spelled out. People should be punished according to the law. The Nazis violated this principle with ex post facto laws. In addition to the ex post facto law that imposed a death sentence on Lubbe for burning down the Reichstag building, the Nazis eventually enacted more than 20 ex post facto laws.

The Nazis went beyond ex post facto laws. Instead of making the criminal law clear, they introduced vagueness. In 1935, the Criminal Code was amended to read: "A person will be punished who commits an act that the law declares to be punishable or that deserves punishment according to . . . healthy public opinion." In other words, a person could be punished because judges believed he deserved punishment. In a speech to judges, Joseph Goebbels, the Nazi minister of propaganda, said that their decisions should "be based less on law than on the fundamental idea that lawbreakers are to be eliminated from the community of the people."

The courts added to the vagueness of the criminal law by interpreting it to ensure convictions. For example, the pianist Karlrobert Kreiten on tour in Berlin had dinner with a friend of his mother. The woman was an ardent Nazi. To annoy her, he called Hitler "brutal, sick, and insane." She reported him to the authorities. He was charged in People's Court with violating the Decree of Martial Law. This law imposed the death penalty for anyone who "publicly attempts to paralyze or undermine the will of the German or an allied nation to defend itself." The court used tortured logic to show how Kreiten's actions violated this law. For instance, the law required the attempt be public. Yet the conversation had taken place in a private home with only the two of them present. The court explained that the remark was made in public "because everyone must reckon with the fact that German citizens who hear something like this . . . will report it to the authorities . . . ." Kreiten was tried and convicted on September 3, 1943 and executed four days later.

Police Investigations

In democratic societies, laws regulate police behavior. Rules restrict who the police may search and arrest. Police must follow guidelines in questioning suspects.

In Nazi Germany, the Gestapo could do whatever it wanted. One court even ruled that the Reichstag Fire Decree had gotten rid of "all federal and state limitations on police measures." Members of the Gestapo could search and arrest whomever they wanted. Without permission, they opened mail and wiretapped phones. They routinely tortured suspects to extract confessions and information from them.

The regular police were not supposed to use torture, but suspects often appeared in court showing signs of torture. New rules for police formalized the practice. The rules limited beatings, but did not cover torture techniques such as depriving prisoners of food, water, sunlight, and sleep. These rules did not apply to the Gestapo, and the regular police routinely ignored them.

Judicial Independence

Another basic legal principle is judicial independence. Judges should interpret and apply the law free of outside influence. Politics should not sway them. Many countries give judges long terms in office to ensure judicial independence. The U.S. Constitution, for example, gives federal judges life tenure.

Germany had a long history of judicial independence. The Nazis rejected the practice. German legal scholar Carl Schmitt declared that judges must interpret the law "according to National Socialism."

In April 1933, a civil service law expelled Jews, Social Democrats, and those "politically unreliable" from the bench. Judges were expected to serve the Nazi state. Those who did not were removed from office.

To further inject National Socialism into the judiciary, the Nazi state created two new courts—the Special Courts and the People's Court. The People's Court consisted of two judges and five Nazi Party officials. Membership in the Nazi Party was required of all judges on Special Courts.

A defendant stands before the People's Court. Like many others, he was condemned to death.

The People's Court and Special Courts handled political crimes, which eventually accounted for most criminal offenses. The Special Courts dealt with all crimes committed in Nazi-occupied territory during World War II.

The criminal procedures in these new courts served as models for all courts. The "simplified" procedures did away with the rights of the accused. They set up assembly-line justice, with one summary proceeding following another.

The role of defense attorneys was changed. They were expected to work with prosecutors and judges to pursue the interests of the state. The minister of justice sent a "Letter to Lawyers" explaining: "As counsel for the defense, the attorney has taken up a position closer to the state and the community. He has . . . lost his earlier position as a one-sided representative of the defendant."

The courts decided what evidence to hear, and the prosecution did not have to produce much evidence to convince the court of a defendant's guilt. In one case before a Special Court, a Pole named Ignatz Kazmierczak was charged with stabbing a German police dog. No one had witnessed the crime. The Special Court stated that "the guilt of the accused is based on the following facts."

> When the accused was arrested on August 4, 1940, the witness Knippel brought along his injured dog. On seeing the dog, the accused became alarmed. . . . The dog . . . immediately became enraged and set upon the accused. The defendant's behavior proves that he is the one who stabbed the dog, what is more the dog recognized the accused at once as his enemy.

Based on this evidence, Kazmierczak was found guilty, sentenced to death, and executed.

Sentences were carried out immediately. Defendants lost their right to appeal. But if a court found a defendant not guilty, prosecutors could appeal the verdict. This practice violated the principle against double jeopardy. In democratic societies, when a person is found not guilty, that person cannot be tried again for the same crime. Nazi Germany did not honor the protection against double jeopardy.

In fact, if a person were acquitted or released from jail, the person might be arrested by the Gestapo and sent to a concentration camp. This practice violated not only the principle against double jeopardy, but also the principle that only the judiciary could try and sentence offenders. Seeing the Gestapo cart away people even enraged Nazi judges and the Ministry of Justice because it was seen as an attack on their authority. They finally got the Gestapo to agree to make their arrests outside the courtroom to spare them embarrassment.

In one instance, Hitler even declared himself the "supreme judge." In 1934, he purged the leaders of the Storm Troopers, his paramilitary group. The purge, known as the Night of the Long Knives, was a weekend massacre. Hitler had ordered the Storm Trooper leadership to meet at a hotel. Hitler and SS troops moved in, seized, and shot the leaders. Hitler admitted to killing almost 80, but probably hundreds died in the violent attacks. A one-sentence law was passed that made the murders legal: "The measures taken on June 30 and July 1 and 2, 1934, to put down attacks of high treason shall be legal state self-defense." (Law Concerning Measures for the Defense of the State, July 1934). Hitler justified his actions in a speech to the Reichstag: "If anyone reproaches me and asks why we did not call upon the regular courts for sentencing, my only answer is this: In that hour, I was responsible for the fate of the German nation and was thus the supreme judge of the German people."

Punishments

Another basic principle is that the punishment should fit the crime. In the United States, for example, only a person convicted of murder can be sentenced to death. In 1932, the year before Hitler took power, Germany only allowed the death sentence for three crimes. By 1939, the year that World War II began, the number of crimes carrying the death penalty had risen to 46. All criminals came to be considered enemies of the state.

German courts frequently handed down the death penalty, especially during the war. They liberally interpreted when it should be applied. For example, when Werner Hollander, a young Hungarian living in Germany, applied for a job with a German arms manufacturer, his ancestry was checked. It was revealed that he had Jewish ancestors, a fact he had not known. It was against the law for Jews to have sexual relationships with Germans. Hollander was charged with violating the law. This law did not carry the death penalty, but because Hollander had had several relationships during his time in Germany, he was charged with being a habitual offender. This was a capital crime intended for serious repeat offenders. He was convicted and executed.

Courts sentenced an astounding number of defendants to death. The courts in Germany sentenced about 40,000 to 50,000 to death. German military courts executed another 10,000 as of mid-1944 (when the official count stopped). In occupied areas, the Special Courts ordered another 80,000 executed. These numbers do not include the millions murdered in death camps in the Holocaust. In comparison, Germany's allies carried out few executions. The Italian military courts sentenced just 29 to die. Only two people in Japan were sentenced to death by civilian courts.

Equal Treatment

Another basic legal principle is that all people should treated equally under the law. No one should be discriminated against because of race, creed, or national origin. This principle went against the Nazi ideology of racism. Nazi laws and courts openly discriminated against those belonging to particular races, religions, and nationalities. The Nuremberg Laws of 1935 outlawed marriages between Jews and Germans, banned sexual contact between them, and stripped Jews of German citizenship.

German courts treated harshly any criminal defendant who was a Jew, Russian, Pole, gypsy, or Jehovah's Witness. The German Supreme Court expressed the Nazi view:

> The earlier (liberal) view of personal rights made no fundamental distinction among human beings on the basis of sameness or difference in blood . . . . According to the National Socialist world view, however, only individuals of German heritage (and those placed on an equal legal footing with them) should be treated as persons with full legal rights within the German state.

For Discussion

1. German legal scholar Carl Schmitt, a Nazi sympathizer, wrote: "Today everyone will recognize that the maxim 'No crime without punishment' takes priority over 'No punishment without law' as the higher and stronger legal truth." What do the two maxims mean? Which do you think has the greater "legal truth"? Why?

2. What were the basic principles that Nazi justice violated? Give examples of how the principles were violated. Which violations did you find most offensive? Why?

ACTIVITY

The Need for an Independent Judiciary

Writing in the 17th century, the French philosopher Montesquieu emphasized the need for government to separate its executive, legislative, and judicial powers. When the U.S. Constitution was written in the next century, the U.S. founders followed Montesquieu's advice and formed three branches of government. The founders especially recognized a need for an independent judiciary free from political influence. To ensure judicial independence, the Constitution set life terms for all federal judges.

The Nazi regime rejected the idea of judicial independence. It intentionally eliminated the independence of the judiciary in order to bring about Nazi "justice."

Write an essay on this topic: Why is an independent judiciary necessary? Cite examples from the experience of Nazi Germany to bolster your argument.

The Plot to Assassinate Hitler

By the early 1940s, Hitler had enemies within his high command plotting to kill him. The leader of the main plot was Colonel Claus von Stauffenberg. In 1926, he had joined the German cavalry. He was promoted to first lieutenant in 1933, the year Hitler made his move to seize power in Germany.

As a young officer, Stauffenberg held no strong political beliefs. He refused to join with his fellow officers when they ridiculed the weak Weimar Republic. Nor was he attracted to the Nazi Party or its charismatic leader, Adolf Hitler. Stauffenberg did believe that the German army had a mission to protect Germany and guard the good reputation of the German people.

When Hitler became dictator, Stauffenberg, along with most other Germans, hoped for a new era of political and economic stability. He joined with all other members of the German army in swearing the following oath of loyalty to the new leader:

> I swear by Almighty God this sacred oath: I will render unconditional obedience to the Fuehrer of the German Reich and people, Adolf Hitler, Supreme Commander of the Army, and, as a brave soldier, I will be ready at any time to stake my life for this oath.

A High Noble Purpose

Between 1936 and 1938, Stauffenberg received additional training at the Army Staff College where he was promoted to captain. Although he had a low regard for Hitler (Stauffenberg called him "the wallpaper hanger"), the 31-year-old captain followed orders and went to war.

By 1942, many top military officers viewed the invasion of the Soviet Union as a terrible mistake. Hitler took over direct command of the military. As supreme commander, he insisted on attacks along the Russian front despite heavy losses. Hitler's generals followed orders, but increasingly grumbled behind his back. Stauffenberg grew convinced that Hitler was leading Germany to disaster.

German army Colonel Claus von Stauffenberg was the leader of a plot to kill Hitler. It almost succeeded.

Stauffenberg began searching for army generals willing to take part in a military coup, a takeover of Hitler's government. Many generals sympathized with Stauffenberg's aims, but few were willing to act. When Hitler ordered his troops to hold out at Stalingrad despite huge losses, Stauffenberg decided that the fuehrer must be removed so that Germany could live.

For Discussion

1. Who was Claus von Stauffenberg?

2. What prompted him to act against Hitler?

ACTIVITY

Oaths

Stauffenberg swore a personal oath of loyalty to Hitler in 1934. Everyday, people swear oaths or make promises. Is it ever justified to break an oath or promise?

In your group, do the following:

1. Discuss the situation you are assigned.
2. Examine the reasons for keeping the oath or promise.
3. Examine the reasons for breaking it.
4. Decide whether or not the person would be justified in breaking it.
5. Prepare to report to the class on your decision and your reasons for it.

Situations

A. Stauffenberg swore a personal oath of loyalty to Hitler in 1934. Was he justified in plotting the death of his military commander and national leader nine years later?

B. A father witnesses his 23-year-old son shoot a man to death. The father is called as a witness at the son's trial. Would he be justified in saying that he did not see the shooting?

C. A leader of a country promises to send troops to help one side of a civil war in another country. The war drags on. Is the leader justified in removing his country's troops?

D. Sam is a member of a national security agency. He took an oath not to reveal information labeled "secret" to those not authorized to see this information. He finds a secret document showing that the government is engaged in illegal spying. He goes to his superior who tells him to ignore the document. Is he justified in leaking the document to the press?

E. Julie makes Maria promise she will tell no one what she is about to tell her. Maria promises. Julie tells her she is going to poison her husband the next day. Would Maria be justified in breaking her promise?

F. At their wedding five years ago, Jamie and Samuel vowed to each other "to have and to hold from this day forward, for better or for worse, for richer, for poorer, in sickness and in health, to love and to cherish; from this day forward until death do us part." Now Samuel is tired of all the bickering with his wife. Would Samuel be justified in breaking his vow and seeking a divorce?

The Hitler Plot Trials

Stauffenberg was promoted and sent to fight in North Africa. He suffered injuries resulting in the loss of his left eye, right hand, and two fingers of his left hand. During his long recovery, Stauffenberg came to believe that God had allowed him to live to serve a noble purpose. He concluded he must assassinate Hitler.

By the summer of 1943, Stauffenberg was transferred to army headquarters in Berlin. The city of Berlin was becoming the center of a growing conspiracy to get rid of Hitler. In fact, during the spring of 1943, two others had tried to kill Hitler. The attempts had failed.

Stauffenberg became the driving force behind the latest plot. In Paris, conspirators even tried to enlist into the plot Field Marshal Erwin Rommel, a German military hero. By 1944, Stauffenberg was chief of staff to General Friedrick Fromm. Fromm knew about Stauffenberg's involvement in the conspiracy, but he neither joined the plot nor turned his subordinate over to the Gestapo.

On July 19, 1944, Stauffenberg had his chance to kill Hitler. He was ordered to attend a briefing at Hitler's military headquarters, called Wolf's Lair, located in what is now Poland.

The briefing was taking place in a hut. Stauffenberg entered the hut and sat down. Hitler was leaning over a massive table covered with maps. Cautiously, Stauffenberg placed his briefcase containing a bomb under the heavy table and slipped out of the room unnoticed. Just before he drove off, he heard an explosion from inside the briefing hut. It was 12:45 p.m.

Stauffenberg could see clouds of smoke billowing from the briefing hut. In the confusion, he escaped, convinced that the fuehrer had died.

Inside the hut, the explosion had thrown everyone to the floor. Four army officers were killed, but the heavy table protected Hitler. With only minor injuries, he walked out of the briefing hut in a daze. Hitler lived.

In this Berlin courtyard, Stauffenberg and three other plotters were executed.

The Plot Fails

At 6:45 p.m., six hours after the assassination attempt, a German radio station finally broadcast this bulletin:

> A bomb attack was made upon the fuehrer today. . . . The fuehrer was unhurt apart from minor burns and contusions. He continued with his work forthwith and, as arranged, received the Duce [Mussolini] for a lengthy discussion . . . .

Gradually, Stauffenberg and the other conspirators learned that Hitler had survived the bombing. Some abandoned the effort and attempted to protect themselves. Most, including Stauffenberg, decided to go ahead and try to overthrow Hitler's government. But the bulk of army officers and civilians refused to back the coup with Hitler still alive.

Troops loyal to Hitler invaded the office building in Berlin where Stauffenberg had set up his headquarters. Shots were fired and Stauffenberg was wounded in his one good arm.

General Fromm accused Stauffenberg and four other officers of treason and condemned them to death. The general allowed one of the five condemned men to shoot himself in the head. About 10 p.m., he ordered the others outside to be shot in a courtyard illuminated by armored car headlights.

The Trials

Early the next morning, Hitler spoke to the German people on the radio. He called the conspirators "a gang of criminal elements" and promised that they would be "destroyed without mercy." Hitler kept his promise.

The Gestapo began to arrest hundreds of army officers and civilians. Some innocent people fell into the trap. Others who were guilty escaped. A few took their own lives. One officer put a grenade in his mouth and pulled the pin.

Initially a few hundred people were arrested. But as time went on, the Nazis found out that the plot involved many more. Before the end of the war, the Gestapo had arrested thousands in connection with the plot.

Heinrich Himmler, then in charge of the SS and Gestapo, called for the ancient German custom of blood responsibility for Stauffenberg. "This man has committed treason. His blood is bad. There is traitor's blood in him that must be wiped out. And the entire family was wiped out down to the last member. And so too will Count Stauffenberg's family be wiped out down to the last member."

The Gestapo took into custody Stauffenberg's wife, brothers, their wives, children, and cousins. Most were sent to concentration camps. The Gestapo arrested family members of other plotters, even small children. All were assumed to be guilty and subject to execution.

Hitler wanted show trials for those in the military who had plotted against him. He declared: "This time I will make short work of them. . . . They will come before the People's Court. They will not be allowed to speak at all, and the sentence must be carried out immediately, within two hours of its pronouncement. They will hang at once . . . ."

The head judge of the People's Court was Roland Freisler. Hitler said: "Freisler will take care of it. He is our Vishinsky." He was referring to Andrei Vishinsky, the chief prosecutor at Stalin's show trials in the 1930s.

The first of many trials took place on August 7 and 8, 1944. Like all the other trials, it was a sham. No defense evidence or cross-examination of witnesses was permitted, and the Gestapo's evidence went unchallenged.

The defendants were four generals, four other officers, and a few people not in the military. All had been tortured and looked beaten-up. One officer had been given pants much too large and no belt to them it up. As he held up his pants, Freisler barked at him: "You dirty old man, why are you always fiddling with your pants?"

Freisler dominated the trial. Refusing to let the defendants utter more than a few words, he heaped insults on them. He called them "rabble," "criminals," and "traitors." To one, he said: "A rat is what you are. You should be stepped on, squashed flat."

The defendants were assigned attorneys, but they could not consult with them. That did not matter, because their attorneys supported the prosecution. One defense attorney said in his concluding remarks to the court, "The deed of the accused stands, and the guilty perpetrator will go down with it."

All were sentenced to hang. Hitler had ordered: "They should hang like slaughtered cattle." They were hanged on meat hooks.

On August 10, four more defendants were tried. Even though all defendants had been tortured, they refused to repent for their actions. In court, they often blurted out accusations against Hitler. One stated: "We resolved to take this deed upon ourselves in order to save Germany from indescribable misery. I realize that I shall be hanged for my part in it, but I do not regret what I did and only hope that someone else will succeed under luckier circumstances." Another commented on "all the murders committed at home and abroad." The behavior of the defendants did not please Hitler. On August 17, he decided to stop all reporting on the trials.

But the trials continued for months. One was held about every two weeks. On February 3, 1945, the court took refuge in a basement during an air raid. A direct hit on the courthouse caused the shelter ceiling to fall. Only one person was injured. A beam struck Judge Freisler, killing him.

The death of Freisler ended the trials in the People's Court. Hitler ordered all suspects transferred to concentration camps. There the SS conducted "trials" and executions. In a twist of irony, General Fromm, the man who had ordered Stauffenberg to be shot, also found himself accused. Found guilty of failing to act soon enough against the conspirators, he was shot on March 12, 1945.

Because of Rommel's popularity with the German people, Hitler decided not to put him on trial. Instead, Rommel agreed to end his own life by taking poison.

Most of those executed died by hanging or strangulation. The executions were all filmed so Hitler would have the ghoulish pleasure of seeing his enemies die. The last hanging took place on April 20, 1945, Hitler's birthday. About 5,000 persons had been executed.

Today in a cemetery outside Berlin is a memorial chapel dedicated to Claus von Stauffenberg and the others who plotted the death of Adolf Hitler. An inscription in the chapel reads: "They resisted the enemies of their nation and gave their lives for the maintenance of the law of God."

For Discussion

1. How did Stauffenberg's plot fail?
2. What happened to General Fromm? Do you think it was just? Explain.
3. Hitler wanted show trials of the military plotters. What were the trials like? How were these trials different from the Soviet show trials?

ACTIVITY

Forms of Opposition

Many historians view the plot as being a case of too little, too late. In a speech, former U.S. Secretary of State Alexander Haig once reflected on Germany's tragic experience leading up to the Holocaust. He urged the citizens of all nations to be on constant alert for what he called "signposts on the road to tyranny" and to take prompt action if their governments act repressively or unlawfully. This raises a question: What form of opposition should you take, if any, when your government violates basic principles of human rights?

Imagine you are a citizen of a country in which the following events take place. Working in groups, decide for each:

1. Would you oppose the governmental action? Why or why not?
2. What would you do? Why?

Be prepared to present and discuss your conclusions with the class.

Events

1. Your government breaks an international treaty with its neighboring country and seizes 200 square miles of territory.
2. Your government suspends its national constitution and disbands all competing political parties.
3. Your government suspends the individual rights of its citizens and makes mass arrests.
4. Your national leader diverts millions of dollars from the treasury and uses it for a luxurious lifestyle.
5. Your national leader makes a speech calling for the segregation of a minority group in special housing zones.

Unit 6
War Crimes

In World War I, troops wait in trenches prepared for a poison-gas attack.

The Hague Conventions

At the turn of the 20th century, two trends in warfare troubled many military experts. First, weapons were becoming much more deadly. Huge cannons, repeating rifles, machine guns, and poison gas could turn battlefields into arenas of mass slaughter. Second, it was becoming difficult to avoid civilian casualties. One reason was the powerful new weapons coming into use. Their destructive force could not be contained within battle zones. The changing nature of war also contributed. More wars were being fought with guerrilla fighters wearing civilian clothing, and many soldiers justified killing civilians because they could be, and probably were, enemy guerrilla fighters.

Recognizing that wars would probably continue to occur, most European nations sent diplomats to a series of conferences at The Hague, a city in Holland, to draw up "rules of war." In 1899 and again in 1907, diplomats met to write conventions, or agreements, that would outlaw the unnecessary suffering of prisoners of war and wounded soldiers. The Hague Conventions also attempted to protect civilians and non-military targets during wartime.

Vocabulary

Auschwitz (OUSH witz) The site of the largest Nazi concentration camp, located in southern Poland.

Burundi (bə REWN dē) A country in east central Africa surrounded by Rwanda on the north, Tanzania on the east and south, and the Republic of Congo on the west.

Geneva (jə NĒ və) A city in Switzerland that has been the site of many international conferences.

genocide (JEN ə sīd) n. The planned killing of a whole racial, ethnic, or religious group.

Hutu (HEW tew) n. An ethnic group in Rwanda and Burundi.

Khmer Rouge (KEM ər REWZH) n. A Cambodian Communist revolutionary movement that controlled the country from 1975–79. (*Khmer* refers to the largest ethnic group in Cambodia. *Rouge* is French for "red.")

Rwanda (rə WON də) A country in east central Africa surrounded by Uganda on the north, Tanzania on the east, and the Republic of Congo on the west.

Srebrenica (sre bre NĒT sə) A small mountain town in Bosnia and Herzegovina.

The Hague (*th*ə HĀG) The capital city of the Netherlands.

tribunal (trī BŪ nəl) n. A court of justice.

Tutsi (TEWT sē) n. An ethnic group in Rwanda and Burundi.

unilateral (ūn ə LAT ə rəl) adj. Acting alone instead of in concert with other nations.

vigilante group (vij ə LAN tē GREWP) n. Persons who illegally take the law into their own hands and punish suspected lawbreakers.

Pronunciation Key: bat, āte, are, däre, den, ēgo, **new**, **her**, bit, īce, îrritate, box, nō, **born**, **oil**, **out**, but, ūse, **chum**, **she**, **thin**, ***th*e**, **zh** sound in trea**su**re or mira**g**e; **ə** is the **uh** sound in unaccented syllables.

The Hague Conventions were among the first attempts to write rules of war into international law. The most important agreement, The Hague Convention on the Laws and Customs of War on Land in 1907, placed many restrictions on nations involved in warfare. In effect, the Hague Conventions created war crimes under international law.

After World War I, nations again attempted to bring an end to the horrors of war. The League of Nations was formed (without the United States) to encourage peace through international cooperation. In 1928, many countries including the United States tried to outlaw war by signing the Kellogg-Briand Treaty. It required those countries signing the pact to foreswear the use of armed violence as an instrument of national policy.

For Discussion

1. What trends in warfare troubled military experts at the beginning of the 20th century?
2. What are the Hague Conventions? What did they try to outlaw?
3. Do you think rules of war are possible? Explain.

Excerpts From International Treaties Setting "Rules of War"

From The Hague Convention on the Laws and Customs of War on Land (1907)

- Prisoners of war "must be humanely treated."
- It "is especially forbidden" to:
  - "employ poison or poisoned weapons."
  - "kill or wound an enemy who, having laid down his arms, or having no longer means of defence, has surrendered . . ."
  - "employ arms, projectiles, or material calculated to cause unnecessary suffering . . . ."
- "The attack or bombardment, by whatever means, of towns, villages, dwellings, or buildings which are undefended is prohibited."
- "Until a more complete code of the laws of war has been issued, the High Contracting Parties deem it expedient to declare that, in cases not included in the Regulations adopted by them, the inhabitants and the belligerents remain under the protection and the rule of the principles of the law of nations, as they result from the usages established among civilized peoples, from the laws of humanity, and the dictates of the public conscience."

From Convention on the Prevention and Punishment of the Crime of Genocide (1948)

"The Contracting Parties confirm that genocide, whether committed in time of peace or in time of war, is a crime under international law which they undertake to prevent and to punish."

From Geneva Conventions on the Law of War (1949)

- "Persons taking no active part in the hostilities, including members of armed forces who have laid down their arms and those placed hors de combat [out of action] by sickness, wounds, detention, or any other cause, shall in all circumstances be treated humanely . . . . To this end, the following acts are . . . prohibited . . . : (a) violence to life and person, in particular murder of all kinds, mutilation, cruel treatment and torture; (b) taking of hostages; (c) outrages upon personal dignity . . . ."
- "Every prisoner of war . . . is bound to give only his surname, first names and rank, date of birth, and army, regimental, personal or serial number . . . ."
- ". . . prisoners of war must at all times be protected, particularly against acts of violence or intimidation and against insults and public curiosity."

From Convention Against Torture and other Cruel, Inhuman or Degrading Treatment or Punishment (1984)

". . . no one shall be subjected to torture or to cruel, inhuman or degrading treatment or punishment . . . ."

ACTIVITY

Rules of War

Imagine that your group is a committee at an international conference on the rules of war. Your committee's task is to come up with ideas for rules of war. Your ideas will be voted on by the full convention. Do the following as a group:

1. Choose one person to record your ideas.
2. Reread the article together. Think of rules of war to address problems discussed in the article. Have the recorder write them down.
3. Read together the "Excerpts From International Treaties Setting 'Rules of War' " on page 92. Discuss these questions:
   - Which of these rules, if any, do you agree with?
   - Which, if any, do you disagree with?
   - Which do you think are most important? Least important?

   Again, have the recorder write down your responses.
4. Select the three rules that you think are most important. Select a person to report the rules (and your reasons for them) to the convention.

The Nuremberg Tribunal

In spite of efforts to prevent war, in 1939, war again engulfed the world. World War II proved to be even more horrifying than World War I, especially with regard to the treatment of civilians.

Between the years 1933, when Adolf Hitler came to power in Germany, and 1945, when World War II ended, the Nazis arrested, deported to concentration camps, and systematically murdered an estimated 6 million European Jews. These actions annihilated nearly 70 percent of the Jewish population of Europe. Millions of non-Jews who the Nazis considered to be "undesirables" also died in concentration camps.

The worst of the death camps, Auschwitz, was located in Nazi-occupied Poland. Death came to the prisoners of Auschwitz in gruesome ways: by shooting, starvation, poisoning, and torture. Many died from cruel medical experiments conducted by German doctors. In addition, the Nazis gassed thousands of people to death in underground chambers each day. The statistics of death are staggering. Fifty ovens were kept busy burning 10,000 bodies each 24-hour period. Workers dumped the ashes in a nearby river. Unburned bones, the hair, and any personal effects of the victims were sold to aid the German war effort. A total of 4 million men, women, and children died at Auschwitz alone.

After the war ended, the Big Four, the United States, the United Kingdom, France, and the Soviet Union, acted together to try 22 German Nazi military and government leaders for their crimes. (Hitler had committed suicide.) For the first time, the war leaders of a defeated nation would be prosecuted under international law to enforce the "rules of war." An international tribunal was set up at Nuremberg, Germany. Each of the four Allied powers appointed two judges to the panel conducting the trial.

The 22 Nazi leaders were charged with crimes under international law including "war crimes" and "crimes against humanity." Actions listed as war crimes included the killing, torture, and enslavement of prisoners of war and civilians in violation of the laws and customs of war. Under crimes against humanity, the former leaders of Nazi Germany were accused of carrying out a policy of persecution, deportation, enslavement, and murder of various groups including the 6 million Jews who died in Hitler's death camps.

Nuremberg defendants sit in the dock with soldiers standing behind them.

U.S. Supreme Court Justice Robert Jackson acted as chief American prosecutor at the Nuremberg trial. In his opening statement, Jackson said:

> The common sense of mankind demands that law shall not stop with the punishment of petty crimes by little people. It must also reach men who possess themselves of great power and make deliberate and concerted use of it to set in motion national evils which leave no home in the world untouched. . . .

Jackson set out to establish that national leaders should be held responsible and punished for wartime violations of international law. He made the point that this principle should apply to all national leaders for all time, not just those on trial at Nuremberg. "The ultimate step in avoiding periodic wars," declared Jackson, ". . . is to make statesmen responsible to law."

The prosecution took 15 weeks to present its case against the Nazi leaders. The evidence included records carefully kept by the Nazis themselves and films of the death camps.

A team of German lawyers defended the Nazis. They made three main arguments on behalf of the 22 defendants:

1. The Allies also committed war crimes, yet only the defeated Germans were tried. For example, Dresden, a historic German city known for its architectural beauty, was mercilessly destroyed by British and American bombers only a few weeks before the end of the war. About 25,000–35,000 persons, mostly civilians, died in the air raids.

2. The criminal acts charged against the German leaders were legal under Nazi law. Hitler, ruling by decree, had ordered the concentration camps and the extermination of certain groups of people. Even under international law, none of these acts was specifically held to be illegal. Furthermore the defense lawyers argued that the Nuremberg tribunal had no right to create international crimes for acts after they were committed.

3. All decisions and orders in Nazi Germany originated with one man: Adolf Hitler. The defense lawyers claimed that none of the 22 defendants really had any say in this one-man government. They only followed orders. Only Hitler could be held responsible, and he was dead.

The Nuremberg judges rejected all these arguments. The judges pointed out that although the Hague Conventions and other treaties did not specifically mention concentration camps and the extermination of groups, the wording and intent clearlycovered such acts. Furthermore, reasoned the judges, international law is based not only on written treaties, but also on common customs and practices followed by most nations. The international tribunal concluded, "war crimes (and crimes against humanity) were committed on a vast scale never before seen in the history of war."

As for the question of responsibility, the tribunal judges refused to accept the argument that only Hitler could be blamed. The judges declared, "Any person who commits an act which constitutes a crime under international law is responsible and therefore liable to punishment."

The tribunal dealt with the defense argument about following orders, "The fact that a person acted pursuant to orders of his government or of a superior does not relieve him from responsibility under international law, provided a moral choice was in fact possible to him."

Of the 22 defendants put on trial at Nuremberg, 20 were convicted. Eleven of these men were hanged on October 16, 1946. Hermann Goering, also sentenced to death, committed suicide in his cell the night before he was to hang.

A similar trial of high-ranking Japanese military and civilian leaders took place in Tokyo between 1946 and 1948. In addition, another 185 German military and civilian officials, death camp commanders and doctors, Nazi judges, and businessmen who exploited slave labor were prosecuted in a series of trials at Nuremberg lasting until 1949. The most important legacy of these trials was that for the first time those guilty of perpetrating heinous acts with no military purpose were called to account and punished by a court of international law.

For Discussion

1. Who set up the Nuremberg tribunal? What was its purpose? What was the result of the tribunal?

2. Do you think the Nuremberg tribunal was justified in trying people for war crimes? Explain.

3. Do you think any Allied actions during the war should have been prosecuted as violations of the Hague Conventions? Why?

4. Do you think the Soviet Union, a totalitarian regime, should have been a part of the Nuremberg tribunal? Explain.

ACTIVITY

Since Nuremberg

One purpose of the Nuremberg trials was to hold war criminals responsible for their acts. Since Nuremberg, many wars have been fought, and each has had allegations of war crimes. Below is a list of some recent conflicts. Your group has been assigned one of these conflicts. Do the following:

1. Research the conflict at the library or on the Internet. A good place to begin your Internet research is at **www.crf-usa.org**. Click on Links, *Of Democrats & Dictators* Links, and War Crimes. You will find links to articles about each conflict. Be sure to use several sources for your research because accusations of war crimes are often quite controversial.

2. Find out and make a report explaining:
   - What the conflict was (is) about.
   - What allegations of war crimes have been made.
   - What, if anything, was done to investigate and prosecute the alleged war crimes.

Conflicts

Indonesia Coup (1965–66)

Vietnam War (1968–1973)

Bangladesh War (1971)

Invasion of East Timor (1975)

Cambodian Civil War (1975–1979)

Iran-Iraq War (1980–1988)

Ugandan Civil War (1987–present)

Lebanon Civil War (1975–1990)

Bosnian War (1992–1995)

Iraq's Invasion of Kuwait (1990)

Liberia and Sierra Leone civil wars (1990–2003)

Rwanda (1994)

Darfur Conflict (2003–present)

War in Iraq (2003–present)

The International Criminal Court

Representatives from the member nations meet to discuss the International Criminal Court.

Since the Nuremberg and Tokyo war crimes trials, most countries have signed international agreements outlawing war crimes. In 1948, the U.N. General Assembly voted to prohibit genocide, which it defined as "acts committed with intent to destroy, in whole or part, a national, ethnical, racial, or religious group." Also, the Geneva Conventions of 1949 identified specific crimes against POWs and other non-combatants during wartime. But until recently these additions to international law were never applied.

The reason was not that incidents of genocide stopped. Many appalling atrocities took place. For example, in 1965, the Indonesian army along with civilian vigilante groups slaughtered a half-million Communist Party members, atheists, and foreigners. In 1972, in the African country of Burundi, the government controlled by the Tutsi minority attempted to exterminate the educated class of the Hutu majority. Up to 200,000 were murdered. During the 1971 civil war in East Pakistan (now Bangladesh), over a million people, mostly civilians, were killed.

The worst case of genocide since World War II took place in Cambodia, a Southeast Asian country. In 1975, a Cambodian Communist revolutionary movement of radical students and peasants, the Khmer Rouge, seized control of the country. Within hours of taking power, the Khmer Rouge drove millions of Cambodians out of the cities, which the new rulers believed were evil creations of the capitalist West. The city dwellers, even the old and sick, were forced to march into the countryside to take up new lives as peasants. Those who resisted were shot. Hundreds of thousands died of exhaustion and starvation. The Khmer Rouge shot anyone even remotely associated with the old regime—civil servants, soldiers, doctors, lawyers, merchants, landowners, Buddhist monks, teachers, high school students. The terror finally ended in 1978 when the Vietnamese army entered Cambodia and overthrew the Khmer Rouge government. Within three years, between 1 and 2 million Cambodians, perhaps 20 percent of the total population, had been annihilated.

In 1994, an incredible slaughter took place in Rwanda. As in neighboring Burundi, the Tutsis and Hutus had hated each other for centuries. Unlike Burundi, a Hutu majority ruled Rwanda. In 1990, the Tutsis revolted in Rwanda. The Hutu government armed militia groups to attack Tutsis and anti-government Hutus. During a 100-day frenzy of bloodletting in 1994, Hutu militias sought out and killed perhaps as many as 800,000 Tutsi men, women, and children. In the words of one Hutu militia member, "We were told to kill them all."

With so many incidents, why haven't war criminals been prosecuted? One answer rings out:

International politics makes it difficult to do. At the end of World War II with Germany and Japan defeated, all the major powers agreed on the decision to try German and Japanese war criminals. But then came the Cold War with the two superpowers—the United States and Soviet Union—squared off in fierce international competition. Each had its own allies and client states. Under these circumstances, it was difficult to get the countries of the world to agree about war crimes and who was guilty of committing them.

When the Cold War ended, the possibility of international cooperation seemed to increase. The terrorist attacks on September 11, 2001 and the war on terrorism have increased the need for international cooperation. But even with increased cooperation among nations, some war crimes—especially those committed in a civil war—may be difficult to prosecute. The genocides in Indonesia, East Pakistan, Burundi, and Cambodia took place during civil wars. There is no "police force" that can enter a country and arrest its suspected war criminals.

This is the current problem in the Darfur region of Sudan, where militias helping the government fight a civil war reportedly have slaughtered tens of thousands of people. Civil war was also the problem in Rwanda and in Bosnia. The Bosnian civil war pitted three ethnic groups against one another—Serbs, Croats, and Muslims. Each side charged the other with atrocities and war crimes. Much attention, however, focused on the side winning the civil war—the Bosnian Serbs.

To carve out a separate state for themselves, Bosnian Serbs adopted a policy of "ethnic cleansing." As Serb fighters moved into a Bosnian Muslim area, they raped and terrorized civilians to force them to flee from their homes. Serbs rounded up military-age Muslim men and boys and held them in detention camps. In 1992, the international press exposed starvation and other mistreatment of these prisoners. Suddenly, many in the world saw the image of concentration camps in Europe once again.

Stung by press criticism, the Bosnian Serbs dismantled many of their prison camps. But in July 1995, when the Bosnian Serb army captured the city of Srebrenica, about 8,000 Muslim men and boys disappeared. Witnesses say that they were all shot and buried in mass graves.

In May 1993, largely at the urging of the United States, the U.N. Security Council authorized an international war crimes tribunal for the former Yugoslavia, which included Bosnia. This was the first such court to be established since Nuremberg. In November 1994, the United Nations also set up a war crimes tribunal for Rwanda.

The Permanent ICC

In 1998, representatives from 120 countries approved establishing a permanent International Criminal Court (ICC). Only seven nations refused to sign the treaty. The United States, which had been a leader in setting up previous international courts, was one of the seven opposing the accord. The Clinton administration cited flaws in the treaty. Perhaps its greatest concern was that anti-American governments might press false charges against U.S. soldiers before the court. Despite the misgivings, President Bill Clinton signed the treaty on December 31, 2000. (This was the deadline for any nation to sign and be included in future decisions about the court.) Clinton advised, however, that the Senate not ratify the treaty until its flaws were fixed. Clinton stated that by signing the treaty, the United States "will be in a position to influence the evolution of the Court."

The Bush administration hardened the U.S. position. It called the treaty fatally flawed and announced it was "unsigning" it. Even so, the required 60 countries had ratified the treaty by April 2002, and the new court was created. It has jurisdiction over any genocide, war crimes, or crimes against humanity committed after July 2002.

The Bush administration threatened to cancel all U.S. peacekeeping missions in Bosnia and other places unless the United States was exempted from the International Criminal Court's jurisdiction. In response, the U.N. Security Council voted to exempt all peacekeepers from prosecution for one year. (This exemption has been renewed annually.)

The Bush administration opposes the ICC. It explains that the United States, as the world's only superpower, does much of the world's peacekeeping. This means its soldiers are at greater risk of being accused of war crimes. President George W. Bush has stated: "As the United States works to bring peace around the world our diplomats and/or soldiers can be dragged into the court. That's very troubling."

The administration points out that the tribunals in Bosnia and Rwanda were under the authority of the U.N. Security Council. The United States and other major powers could have vetoed establishing them in the Security Council. But the ICC lies outside the authority of the Security Council. The United States has no veto over who is prosecuted. The treaty gives this power to the court and the prosecutor. This means, the administration warns, that the court and prosecutor might choose to prosecute Americans for political reasons. In short, stated President Bush's press secretary, "The president thinks the ICC is fundamentally flawed because it puts American servicemen and women at fundamental risk of being tried by an entity that is beyond America's reach, beyond America's laws, and can subject American civilian and military to arbitrary standards of justice."

The administration does not oppose setting up international war crimes tribunals. But it believes this should be done, as it has in the past, by the U.N. Security Council for a particular situation.

Ambassador Pierre-Richard Prosper, of the U.S. Office of War Crimes, has said: "There cannot be a cookie-cutter approach to this problem . . . each conflict is unique and has its own set of problems."

All of America's allies disagree with the American position. They see a need for the court. They say it takes too long and too much money to set up special tribunals. They also think the ICC's existence will help prevent future war crimes.

They further point out that safeguards in the treaty make it highly unlikely that U.S. personnel will ever be prosecuted by the court. For example, the court is forbidden from handling a case if the suspect's country is investigating it. Richard Dicker of Human Rights Watch, an international human rights group, has stated: "[W]hen you add up the superb training for U.S. military personnel and the extensive safeguards in this treaty, the likelihood that a U.S. service member would ever appear before it is remote in the extreme." Critics of the Bush administration's position point out that the safeguards have satisfied the British and French, who also send peacekeepers around the world and do not want political prosecutions.

These critics also say that the court procedures will not be arbitrary. Like previous international tribunals, the court guarantees defendants' rights, such as the right to counsel, the presumption of innocence, and the right to a speedy trial.

Critics think the Bush administration's position has hurt America. An editorial in the *St. Louis Post Dispatch* stated: "Mr. Bush has reinforced his image as a unilateralist and deepened international resentment that the United States will only play by its own rules. In opposing the court, Mr. Bush has joined the ranks of North Korea, China, Iraq, Iran and Russia–hardly the company we like to keep on human rights matters."

William Safire, writing in the *New York Times*, supports the Bush administration's decision. He said that "the agreement empowers a global court to arrest, try and imprison American, Israeli and other citizens of democracies for an undefined crime of 'aggression.' With no Security Council veto to restrain the I.C.C., its prosecutor would surely accede today to an Arab League request to indict Israeli soldiers, and tomorrow to indict any U.S. officeholder or servicemember who dared to offend a local dictator. An international prosecutor, answerable to no nation and unrestrained by any Bill of Rights, is the rest of the world's weapon to bring the too-sovereign superpower to heel. Were we to subject ourselves to the rule of the lawless, no U.S. sailor or president could travel abroad without becoming vulnerable to arrest by a politically motivated prosecutor. Multilateral treaties that weaken the U.S. do not strengthen freedom abroad . . . . In our reluctance to appear imperious, we could all too quickly abdicate leadership by catering to the envious crowd."

The Bush administration hopes that its refusal to participate in the ICC will lead to its demise. Supporters of the court hope that its actions will bring American support.

For Discussion

1. Give some examples of serious war crimes that have occurred since World War II. Why did most of them go unpunished?

2. What is the ICC? What problems is it designed to address? Do you think the ICC is a good idea? Why or why not?

ACTIVITY

Should the U.S. Ratify the ICC Treaty?

Imagine that the treaty creating the International Criminal Court has been brought to the U.S. Senate for ratification.

Your group will role play the Senate Foreign Relations Committee. Your group should:

a. Discuss reasons for supporting the treating.

b. Discuss reasons for opposing the treaty.

c. Vote on whether to recommend that the Senate ratify the treaty or not.

d. Be prepared to present your argument for or against the treaty to the class.

Unit 7
Gandhi and Civil Disobedience

Mohandas K. Gandhi (1869–1948) led India to its independence from Great Britain. His picture appears on Indian money. This is from the 1,000 rupee note.

A Brief History of India

Hinduism is the religion of most Indian people. It originated in India thousands of years ago. As part of their culture and religion, Indians developed a rigid caste system. Individuals were born into specific social and occupational groups and were bound to follow the strict rules of their caste throughout their lives.

The Islamic religion entered India about A.D. 700, when Muslim peoples began a series of invasions from West and Central Asia. The Muslims attempted to impose Islam on the Indian people. They succeeded in creating several strong Muslim kingdoms and empires, but the Muslims always ruled as a religious minority in Hindu India.

In the early 1700s, Hindu revolts and a breakdown in law and order ended the last Muslim empire in India. After that, Hindu and Muslim nobles ruled many small independent kingdoms throughout the country.

By the 1600s, the British and other European Christian nations were making their own inroads into this ancient land. The lucrative spice trade first attracted the Europeans. Queen Elizabeth chartered the British East India Company, a private company of British merchants, giving it a monopoly in trading with India.

Vocabulary

Boers (BORZ) n. The descendants of the Dutch settlers in South Africa.

caste system (KAST SIS təm) n. A rigid system of social class.

civil disobedience (SIV əl DIS ō bē dē əns) n. Non-violent and deliberate breaking of the law in order to change the law or alter government policy.

Hinduism (HIN dew iz əm) n. The major religion of India with many different traditions and beliefs.

Jainism (JĪ niz əm) n. An Indian religion that emphasizes non-violence.

lynch (LINCH) v. To punish an accused person without a legal trial, usually done by mob violence.

Mahatma (mə HOT mə) n. In Hinduism, a title of great respect for a spiritual person. (Sanskrit for "great soul.")

Sanskrit (SAN skrit) n. An ancient language of India and the Hindu religion.

satyagraha (sə TYO grə hə) n. Gandhi's word for his policy of civil disobedience. (From Sanskrit meaning "devotion to truth.")

sepoy (SĒ poi) n. An Indian soldier in the British colonial army.

Thoreau (thə RŌ) Henry David Thoreau (1817–1862), American writer whose essay "Civil Disobedience" influenced Gandhi.

untouchables (un TUCH ə bəlz) n. In India, there were four castes and one group outside the caste system, the untouchables.

Pronunciation Key: bat, **ā**te, **ar**e, d**ä**re, den, **ē**go, **new**, h**er**, bit, **ī**ce, **î**rritate, b**o**x, n**ō**, b**or**n, **oi**l, **ou**t, b**u**t, **ū**se, **ch**um, **sh**e, **th**in, ***th**e*, **zh** sound in trea**su**re or mira**g**e; **ə** is the **uh** sound in unaccented syllables.

In 1613, the Muslim emperor of India granted the company the right to establish trading stations in the Bengal region of northeast India. In addition to spices, the company shipped raw materials (such as cotton) to England and imported English manufactured goods (such as clothing) to sell to the Indian people.

By making treaties with local Indian princes and warlords, the East India Company rapidly controlled more and more Indian territory. By 1849, it had subdued all of India, but allowed Indian kings to rule some areas. Company officials in India made fabulous fortunes, living in huge houses attended by scores of Indian servants.

At first, the East India Company directly ruled British-controlled areas of India, such as Bengal. In 1784, however, the British Parliament put the company under its authority. Even so, the day-to-day administration of law in British India remained in the hands of the company.

The East India Company used three large private armies to protect its property and to expand its control over Indian territory. By 1856, the company employed 300,000 native Indian troops. Most were infantrymen called sepoys. Three-fourths of the sepoys were Hindus, and the rest were Muslims.

Discontent among the Bengal sepoys grew as the Indian people became restless over British rule. Many Indians resisted when the British tried to abolish ancient Hindu customs and caste rules. They resented that the British also encouraged Christian missionaries. Most Hindus and Muslims believed that the British wanted to destroy their religions.

In 1857, a sepoy mutiny sparked a rebellion against the British. When the sepoy mutiny first erupted, the British had only 23,000 regular British army troops in India to restore order. Eventually, the British had to bring in troops from all over their empire to fight the rebels.

For more than a year, the sepoys and their civilian allies desperately fought the British army. By the end of 1858, the British had finally restored order. Queen Victoria pardoned all rebels except those who had murdered British subjects. British troops, however, continued to execute thousands of sepoys and other Indians.

After the uprising, the British Parliament abolished the East India Company and placed the governing of India directly in the hands of the British government. Thus India continued as a British colony.

India did not achieve independence for almost another 100 years. The leader of this successful independence movement–Mohandas K. Gandhi–did not seem like a person destined to lead millions of Indians in their battle for independence. And the tactics that he insisted his followers use in this struggle–non-violent civil disobedience–seemed unlikely to drive a powerful empire from India.

For Discussion

1. The British gradually took over India. How do you think the British justified this takeover? Do you think it was justified? Why or why not?
2. What do you think was the main cause of the uprising against British rule in India?
3. What potential intergroup conflicts do you see in Indian society?

Gandhi's Early Years

Gandhi was born into a Hindu merchant caste family in 1869. He was the youngest child. His father was the chief minister of an Indian province and showed great skill in maneuvering between British and Indian leaders. Growing up, Gandhi exhibited neither his father's interest in politics nor his skill at it. Instead, he was heavily influenced by the Hinduism and Jainism of his devoutly religious mother. She impressed on him beliefs in non-violence, vegetarianism, fasting for purification, and respect for all religions. "Religions are different roads converging upon the same point," he once said.

In 1888, Gandhi sailed for England where, following the advice of his father, he studied to become a lawyer. When he returned to India three years later, he took a job representing an Indian ship-trading company that was involved in a complicated lawsuit in South Africa.

Traveling to South Africa in 1893, Gandhi soon discovered that the ruling white Boers (descendants of Dutch settlers) discriminated against the dark-skinned Indians who had been imported as laborers. Gandhi himself experienced this discrimination when railroad officials ordered him to sit in a third-class coach at the back of a train even though he had purchased a first-class ticket. Gandhi refused the order, and police forced him off the train.

This event changed his life. Gandhi became an outspoken critic of South Africa's discrimination policies. This so angered the Boer population that at one point a white mob almost lynched him.

At the turn of the 20th century, the British fought the Boers over control of South Africa with its rich gold and diamond mines. Gandhi sympathized with the Boers, but sided with Britain because he then believed that the British Empire "existed for the benefit of the world." Britain won the war, but much of the governing

This picture of Gandhi was taken shortly after his arrival in South Africa.

of South Africa remained in the hands of the Boers.

In 1907, the Boer legislature passed a law requiring that all Indians register with the police and be fingerprinted. Gandhi, along with many other Indians, refused to obey this law. He was arrested and put in jail, the first of many times he would be imprisoned for disobeying what he believed to be unjust laws.

While in jail, Gandhi read the essay "Civil Disobedience" by Henry David Thoreau, a 19th-century American writer. Gandhi adopted the term "civil disobedience" to describe his strategy of non-violently refusing to cooperate with injustice, but he preferred the Sanskrit word *satyagraha* (devotion to truth). Following his release from jail, he continued to protest the registration law by supporting labor strikes and organizing a massive non-violent march. Finally, the Boer government agreed to a compromise that ended the most objectionable parts of the registration law.

Having spent more than 20 years in South Africa, Gandhi decided that his remaining life's work awaited him in India. As he left South Africa in 1914, the leader of the Boer government remarked, "The saint has left our shores, I sincerely hope forever."

Gandhi's Return to India

When Gandhi returned to India, he was already a hero in his native land. He had abandoned his Western clothing for the simple homespun dress of the poor people. This was his way of announcing that the time had come for Indians to assert their independence from British domination. Spin and weave, he preached to the Indian masses, and refuse to buy British cloth.

The British had controlled much of India for more than 100 years. Gaining independence would be difficult, because Indians were far from united. Although most Indians were Hindus, a sizeable minority were Muslims. The relationship between the two groups was always uneasy and sometimes violent.

One of Britain's main economic interests in India was to sell its manufactured cloth to the Indian people. As Britain flooded India with cheap cotton textiles, the village hand-spinning and weaving economy in India was crippled. Millions of Indians were thrown out of work and into poverty.

Gandhi struggled throughout his life against what he considered three great evils afflicting India. One was British rule, which Gandhi believed impoverished the Indian people by destroying their village-based cloth-making industry. The second evil was Hindu-Muslim disunity caused by years of religious hatred. The last evil was the Hindu tradition of classifying millions of Indians as "untouchables." Untouchables, those Indians born into the lowest social class, faced severe discrimination and could only practice the lowest occupations.

In 1917, while Britain was fighting in World War I, Gandhi supported peasants protesting unfair taxes imposed by wealthy landowners in the Bihar province in northeastern India. Huge crowds followed him wherever he went. Gandhi declared that the peasants were living "under a reign of terror." British officials ordered Gandhi to leave the province, which he refused to do. "I have disregarded the order," he explained, "in obedience to the higher law of our being, the voice of conscience."

The British arrested Gandhi and put him on trial. But under pressure from Gandhi's crowds of supporters, British authorities released him and eventually abolished the unjust tax system. Gandhi later said, "I declared that the British could not order me around in my own country."

Despite his differences with Britain, Gandhi supported the recruitment of Indian soldiers to help the British war effort. He believed that Britain would return the favor by granting independence to India after the war.

For Discussion

1. What were the major influences on Gandhi in this part of his life?
2. What did Gandhi consider the three greatest evils afflicting India? Why did he consider them evil? Which one do you think would be the hardest to overcome? Why?
3. How did Gandhi justify breaking the law in his civil disobedience campaigns? Do you agree with him? Explain.
4. Why did Gandhi support British recruitment of Indian soldiers for World War I? Do you think he should have? Explain.

Gandhi Against the Empire

Instead of granting India independence after World War I, Britain continued its colonial regime and tightened restrictions on civil liberties. Gandhi responded by calling for strikes and other acts of peaceful civil disobedience. During one protest assembly held in defiance of British orders, colonial troops fired into the crowd, killing more than 350 people. A British general then carried out public floggings and a humiliating "crawling order." This required Indians to crawl on the ground when approached by a British soldier.

The massacre and crawling order turned Gandhi against any further cooperation with the British government. In August 1920, he urged Indians to withdraw their children from British-run schools, boycott the law courts, quit their colonial government jobs, and continue to refuse to buy imported cloth. Now called "Mahatma," meaning "great soul," Gandhi spoke to large crowds throughout the country. "We in India . . . ," he proclaimed, "realize that 100,000 Englishmen need not frighten 300 million human beings."

Many answered Gandhi's call. But as the movement spread, Indians started rioting in some places. Gandhi called for order and canceled the massive protest. He drew heavy criticism from fellow nationalists, but Gandhi would only lead a non-violent movement.

In 1922, the British arrested Gandhi for writing articles advocating resistance to colonial rule. He used his day in court to indict the British Empire for exploiting and impoverishing the Indian people. "In my humble opinion," he declared at his trial, "non-cooperation with evil is as much a duty as is cooperation with good." The British judge sentenced him to six years in prison.

When he was released after two years, Gandhi remained determined to continue his struggle against British colonial rule. He also decided to

Excerpt From Gandhi's Statement to the Court in 1922

. . . I believe that I have rendered a service to India and England by showing in non-co-operation the way out of the unnatural state in which both are living. In my humble opinion, non-co-operation with evil is as much a duty as is co-operation with good. But in the past, non-co-operation has been deliberately expressed in violence to the evil doer. I am endeavouring to show to my countrymen that violent non-co-operation only multiplies evil and that as evil can only be sustained by violence, withdrawal of support of evil requires complete abstention from violence. Non-violent implies voluntary submission to the penalty for non-co-operation with evil. I am here, therefore, to invite and submit cheerfully to the highest penalty that can he inflicted upon me for what in law is a deliberate crime and what appears to me to be the highest duty of a citizen. The only course open to you, the Judge and the Assessors, is either to resign your posts and thus dissociate yourselves from evil if you feel that the law you are called upon to administer is an evil and that in reality I am innocent, or to inflict on me the severest penalty if you believe that the system and the law you are assisting to administer are good for the people of this country and that my activity is therefore injurious to the public weal.

campaign against Hindu-Muslim religious hatred and Hindu mistreatment of the so-called untouchables, whom he called the "Children of God." In Gandhi's mind, all of these evils had to be erased if India were to be free.

In 1930, Gandhi carried out his most spectacular act of civil disobedience. British colonial law made it a crime for anyone in India to possess salt not purchased from the government monopoly. In defiance of British authority, Gandhi led thousands of people on a 240-mile march to the sea where he picked up a pinch of salt. This sparked a mass movement among the people all over the country to gather and make their own salt.

Gandhi was arrested and jailed, but his followers marched to take over the government salt works. Colonial troops attacked the marchers with clubs. But true to Gandhi's principle of non-violence, the protesters took the blows without striking back. Gandhi explained, "I want world sympathy in this battle of Right against Might."

Gandhi now held the attention of the world, which pressured the British to negotiate with Indian leaders on a plan for self-rule. The British, however, stalled the process by making proposals that aggravated Indian caste and religious divisions.

The Mahatma decided that he had to do everything he could to eliminate Hindu prejudice and discrimination against the untouchables if India were ever to become a truly free nation. In 1932, he announced a "fast unto death" as part of his campaign to achieve equality for these downtrodden people. Gandhi ended his fast when some progress was made toward this goal, but he never achieved full equality for the "Children of God."

Gandhi also dreamed of a united as well as a free India. But distrust between the two factions led to increasing calls for partitioning India into separate Hindu and Muslim homelands.

For Discussion

1. What were Gandhi's goals?
2. What non-violent methods did Gandhi use to achieve his goals? Why do you think he insisted on a non-violent movement?

Independence and Assassination

Muslim refugees crowd onto a train leaving India for Pakistan following India's independence from Britain.

During World War II, colonial officials cracked down on a movement calling for the British to "Quit India." They imprisoned Gandhi and many other Indians until the end of the war. Britain's prime minister, Winston Churchill, declared, "I have not become the King's First Minister in order to preside over the liquidation of the British Empire."

When the British people voted out Churchill's government in 1945, Indian independence became inevitable. But the problem was how the Hindu majority and Muslim minority would share power in India. Distrust spilled over into violence between the two religious groups as the Muslims demanded a separate part of India for their own nation, which they would call Pakistan.

Disheartened by the religious hatred and violence, Gandhi spoke to both Hindus and Muslims, encouraging peace and forgiveness. He opposed dividing the country into Hindu and Muslim nations, believing in one unified India.

Finally, in May 1947, British, Hindu, and Muslim political leaders, but not Gandhi, reached an agreement for independence that created a Hindu-dominated India and a Muslim Pakistan. As Independence Day (August 15, 1947) approached, an explosion of Hindu and Muslim looting, rape, and murder erupted throughout the land. Millions of Hindus and Muslims fled their homes, crossing the borders into India or Pakistan.

Gandhi traveled to the areas of violence, trying to calm the people. In January 1948, he announced that he would fast until "a reunion of hearts of all communities" had been achieved. At age 78, he weakened rapidly. But he did not break his fast until Hindu and Muslim leaders came to him pledging peace.

On January 30, 1948, an assassin shot and killed the "great soul" of India while he was attending a prayer meeting. The assassin was a Hindu who believed Gandhi had sold out to the Muslims.

Sadly, the peace he had brokered between Hindus and Muslims did not last. The ancient hatreds remained. War has erupted between India and Pakistan several times, and the two countries remain hostile to one another to this day.

Who was Mahatma Gandhi? He was a physically small man with a big idea who achieved great things. He worked for the dignity of Indians in South Africa, struggled for Indian independence, and inspired others like Martin Luther King Jr. in the United States to confront injustice with non-violent methods. "It is the acid test of non-violence," Gandhi once said, "that in a non-violent conflict there is no rancor left behind and, in the end, the enemies are converted into friends."

For Discussion

1. Do you think Gandhi was a success? Explain.
2. When, if ever, do you think non-violent civil disobedience is justified?
3. Although Gandhi never used or advocated violence, he did not absolutely oppose it. "I do believe that where there is only a choice between cowardice and violence," he wrote, "I would advise violence." Describe a situation where you think Gandhi might agree that resorting to violence was necessary.

ACTIVITY

Non-Violent Civil Disobedience

Since Gandhi, many individuals and groups have employed non-violent civil disobedience. The question has often arisen whether the civil disobedience was justified. In this activity, your group will examine various situations and decide whether the situation calls for civil disobedience.

In your group, discuss each of the situations below. For each, your group should decide two issues:

a. Does the situation justify non-violent civil disobedience? Why or why not?

b. If so, what action would you recommend for those seeking to change the situation? If not, what action would you recommend? Explain your answer.

Be prepared to report your decisions and reasons for them.

Situations

1. In 1955, the year after the U.S. Supreme Court ordered all schools desegregated, most public facilities—hotels, restrooms, water fountains, etc.—remained rigidly segregated in the South. Law remained in Southern states upholding segregation. African Americans were demanding full integration.
2. In 1964 at the University of California in Berkeley, university rules banned all political or religious speakers, fund raising, or recruitment from the campus unless first approved by the campus administration. Students were demanding to exercise what they considered their First Amendment rights to speak out on issues, raise funds for causes, and recruit members of political and religious organizations.
3. In 1967, America was deeply involved in the Vietnam War. Many people believed the war was wrong and demanded that the troops be brought home.
4. In its 1973 *Roe v. Wade* decision, the U.S. Supreme Court in effect legalized abortion in America. Many people today believe abortion is murder and it should be stopped.

Unit 8

International Law

The most important international organization today, the United Nations is headquartered in New York City.

A Brief History of International Law

Much international law took shape in the 20th century. Its roots, however, are long and ancient. Archaeologists have unearthed treaties between two Mesopotamian rulers dating back to 3100 B.C. Egyptian pharaohs also left records of treaties in effect with neighboring peoples. The ancient Chinese created what might be called international law as early as 2500 B.C. Of all ancient peoples, the development of modern international law owes the most to the Romans.

The Law of Rome

From about 31 B.C. to the fifth century A.D., most of Europe was politically united under the Roman Empire. To control the lands conquered by its mighty armies, Rome developed a powerful central administration. Organization, military power, government, and law kept the empire at relative peace for centuries.

To administer justice to diverse peoples, the Romans needed laws that reflected the needs of the empire. Roman judges had to settle disputes among people with different beliefs and languages. To do this, the Romans applied what they called the Law of Nations. It was based on the idea that there is a law that applies to all humans

Vocabulary

archaeology (ar kē OL ə jē) n. The study of humans and their culture through the recovery and examination of artifacts.

bilateral (bī LAT ər əl) adj. Two-sided. A bilateral treaty has two parties.

continental shelf (kon tə NEN təl SHELF) n. The land underwater off the coast before the continental slope, which goes deep to the ocean floor.

Grotius (GRŌ shəs) Hugo Grotius (1583–1645), Dutch legal scholar who wrote the first modern book on international law.

jurisdiction (jer əs DIK shən) n. 1. The authority to apply the law. 2. The range of authority.

League of Nations (LĒG UV NĀ shənz) n. An international organization founded after World War I. It dissolved in 1946 after the United Nations was founded.

maritime (MĂR ə tīm) adj. Having to do with the sea.

multilateral (mul tē LAT ər əl) adj. Many-sided. A multilateral treaty has many parties to it.

original jurisdiction (ə RIJ ə nəl jer əs DIK shən) n. The authority of a court to be the first to hear a case. It is unlike appellate jurisdiction, which authorizes a court to review cases tried by another court.

sovereignty (SOV ər in tē) n. The authority of an independent state.

United Nations (ū NĪ tid NĀ shənz) n. An international organization founded after World War II. Its governing bodies are the Security Council and General Assembly.

uranium (ū RĀ nē əm) n. A heavy metal used in the production of atomic fuel and weapons.

Pronunciation Key: bat, āte, are, däre, den, ēgo, new, her, bit, īce, îrritate, box, nō, born, oil, out, but, ūse, chum, she, thin, *th*e, zh sound in treasure or mirage; ə is the uh sound in unaccented syllables.

regardless of their culture or origin. The Romans developed this system of international law and used it throughout the empire. The law was enforced by the power of Rome.

The Middle Ages

With the breakup of the Roman Empire, Western Europe fell into a period of upheaval and political instability. Threatened by foes from the north and east, people looked for protection from powerful nobles. These unstable political conditions gave rise to the early versions of feudalism, with kings and nobles exercising control over relatively small areas. The local population swore loyalty to a noble or king in exchange for protection and security. During this period, people sought a stabilizing force for bringing order to what, in comparison to the Roman Empire, was a chaotic time.

Of all the institutions of the Middle Ages, the church offered the best chance to fill the role once held by Rome. It could provide a moral voice, even if it were unable to provide the military and political muscle to impose order. Since the church's law applied to all Christians, its law had an international flavor. The sanctity of treaties, the right to make war, and the arbitration of disputes all came under the authority of the pope.

In addition, drawing on Greek and Roman ideas, medieval philosophers contended that there existed a body of legal principles that applied to all people everywhere. They called it "natural law." They believed its rules could be discovered through reasoning. In effect, natural law existed "in the air," merely waiting for the embrace of right-thinking men, no matter what their position in life might be.

The Early Modern Era

The Thirty Years War (1618–1648) ushered in a new era. What began as a religious feud among medieval societies ended with the birth of modern states. To meet the new realities, the doctrine of sovereignty developed. It held that the highest authority rested in the nation-state. Each monarch held authority that once cloaked popes and Roman emperors.

Although the idea of sovereignty addressed the new political reality in Europe, it also raised some thorny questions. If there were no higher authority than the individual states, what authority could regulate them domestically or internationally? If quarrels arose among them, who would settle them? Could monarchs declare war for any reason?

The first answers, philosophically at least, came from the work of Hugo Grotius (1583–1645) and other scholars. Grotius, a Dutch legal scholar, argued for the principle that the actions of states were not above law. Instead, just as individuals were bound by natural law, so were states. He argued that wars could be just or unjust. To decide whether a war was just or unjust, factors such as the motivation of the states and the cause involved had to be considered. From this early scholarship evolved some of our modern ideas about international law.

The Concert of Europe

The French Revolution brought turmoil to France and eventually the Napoleonic wars to much of Europe. When the wars ended with the defeat of Napoleon in 1815, European nations sought stability. Essential to the European political system between 1815 and 1914 was a loose agreement, known as the Concert of Europe, to maintain the "balance of power." European nations formed alliances to ensure that no one power was militarily stronger than another. Stability was maintained, and all-out war was avoided for nearly 100 years. Largely because of its political stability, Europe was able to dictate policy to the rest of the world. International politics and law became Europeanized. Colonial nations were often at a political and legal disadvantage when dealing with European powers.

The rise of nationalism fostered the emergence of the concept of consent. European nations clung to the belief that no state, at least no powerful state, was responsible to any higher authority than itself. International law was thus held to be limited to situations in which a state assented through treaty, accord, or international agreement.

Ultimately, the Concert of Europe, stable for so long, collapsed when alliances dragged the European powers into the First World War.

Collective Security

The 20th century saw two attempts to bring world order through the use of international organizations. After World War I, the League of Nations was formed. And following World War II, the United Nations was established. In both cases, membership was extended to all nations of the world. Both were designed to provide a forum for settling international conflict, a source for international law, and a peacekeeping function through collective security. Under collective security, nations give up the use of force in international disputes and pledge to come to the aid of nations that are attacked by aggressors. Problems arose in defining "aggression" and in getting member nations to agree to act. The rule of law could not escape the reality of politics.

For Discussion

1. Which of the periods mentioned do you think was most important to the development of international law? Why?
2. Many scholars argue that international law is mainly the product of Western thinking. What evidence can you find in the brief history that supports this argument?
3. Who was Hugo Grotius? Why was he important?
4. Do you believe there are universal, or natural, laws? If so, what are they?

What Is International Law?

The International Court of Justice is in The Hague, Netherlands. It hears cases that nations agree to send to it.

Many people question the value of international law. After all, it failed to prevent either of the world wars, and even today war, terrorism, and violence continue to occur. Moreover, international law differs from a national legal system, which has a central authority to make and enforce the law. When one cannot find a similar authority in the international domain, it is tempting to dismiss international law.

Defenders of international law admit that international law has often failed to prevent wars or acts of international terrorism. But they note that domestic laws also often fail to prevent murders or kidnapping. They point out that international law has effectively resolved countless disputes among nations, regional entities, organizations, businesses, and individuals.

A comparison of international law to national law must be carefully made. International law never has been, and perhaps never will be, like national legal systems, because it is much harder to achieve the same level of consensus in the international arena. International law has to function in a world of conflicting values, interests, and experiences.

The philosopher and legal scholar Jeremy Bentham (1748–1832) defined international law as the "body of law governing the legal relationships between states." This definition reflects the traditional view that international law applies only to states (countries), which are in turn responsible for defining and applying law that affects citizens.

A modern definition of international law would define international law to include the regulation of the conduct of international organizations and even individuals in some cases.

Some scholars contend that the whole idea of international law should be rethought. They argue that while there should be global rules and regulations, European and imperialistic countries imposed the current system on the world and that groups of people within current states should have greater legal recognition. They would favor a transnational system of law, in which peoples and groups within nation-states have status and rights under the system.

Sources of International Law

Finding the source of laws in the United States is somewhat difficult. The basic law comes from the U.S. Constitution and its Bill of Rights. On the federal level, there are federal statutes and administrative codes. On the state level, each state has a constitution and the criminal and civil codes. Every city also has ordinances and laws. Finally, federal and state court decisions create a large body of judge-made laws.

Describing the sources of international law is even more difficult. There is no international constitution. Few international codes or statutes exist, and none is universally accepted. Furthermore, no one language expresses the rule of law in the international domain. Where, then, does international law come from? The Statute of the International Court of Justice states that there are four major sources of international law: (1) international custom; (2) international treaties and conventions; (3) general principles of law recognized by civilized nations; and (4) court decisions.

International Custom

Just as there are family or community customs, there are also international customs. A custom is a practice in general use over a long period. When a practice becomes widely accepted by countries within the international community, it takes on the quality of a rule of law. For example, for hundreds of years it was generally accepted that coastal fishing vessels could not be seized as a prize of war. In 1898, during the Spanish-American War, the U.S. government seized two Cuban fishing vessels and sold them at auction. In the 1900 case of the *Paquete Habana* and the *Lola* (175 U.S. 677), the U.S. Supreme Court ruled that the custom against seizing fishing vessels had become a rule of international law and the United States had to follow it.

Treaties and Conventions

A treaty is similar to a contract among nations. It is a formal agreement that establishes rights and duties. For example, if two neighboring countries agree on their national border, they might well formalize it by signing a treaty. A treaty between two countries is called a bilateral treaty. It contributes to international law by describing how a particular issue between them will be managed.

A multilateral treaty is one agreed to by many countries. If enough states sign it and it has worldwide significance, it can create general international law. For example, if a treaty signed by every nation banned the killing of whales, killing whales would violate international law. Even if some countries refused to sign such a treaty, but lived up to its principles anyway, they would still be contributing to the development of general international law. But if a nation refused to sign and continued to kill whales, it would not be normally bound by the treaty. As a general rule, a state must consent before it is subject to a rule of international law. This is often described as the doctrine of consent.

General Principles of Law

General principles of law are found in many legal systems around the world. They can be used as part of legal reasoning by international courts when making a decision about a case. For example, a court might require a nation to act in *good faith* when performing under a treaty or other international obligation. Or a court might order a country to act in a manner consistent with its previous stand on a legal matter.

Court Decisions

Decisions of international courts and even national courts, such as the U.S. Supreme Court, can contribute to the development of international law. When two countries have a case heard by an international court, they often agree in advance to be bound by the decision. When a decision is made, the law is established for that specific case.

The decision can have a broader impact as well. Another court can refer to the decision when dealing with a similar situation. Thus, the first court's opinion takes on the role of a precedent. Of course, the second court may not use the precedent and instead decide the matter in quite a different way. Still, courts are often influenced by the reasoning of a prior court and for the sake of consistency try to follow precedents. In this way, each decision influences the development of law.

National courts also influence the development of international law. This is especially true of the national courts of world powers. For example, the U.S. Constitution gives the Supreme Court original jurisdiction in interpreting treaties ratified by the United States. In fact, Article VI, Section 2, of the Constitution makes treaties the "Supreme Law of the Land." The Supreme Court's precedents guide all U.S. courts. In addition, courts throughout the world will look at U.S. Supreme Court decisions on treaties and may also be influenced. In this way, the court has made a significant contribution to the development of international law.

Other Sources

Other sources also contribute to the development of international law. They include the writings of scholars and international jurists, documents developed by various international law societies, and the declarations, conventions, and resolutions adopted by international organizations such as the United Nations or the Organization of American States (OAS).

The work of the United Nations in developing international law is especially noteworthy. Its International Law Commission has compiled numerous codes of law on specific subject areas. Its declarations have helped define relations among nations and provide standards for human rights around the globe. Its peacekeeping operations have helped develop rules for conflict resolution. In short, the United Nations provides present guidance and greater hope for the future of international law.

The Law and Political Reality

Even if a rule of international law is clearly identified and established, some nations may not obey it. International politics plays a role. In deciding whether or not to consent to the jurisdiction of an international court or to be bound by a treaty, a state weighs the political consequences. Unfortunately for the smooth working of the international legal system, rules or laws may be rejected if they interfere with important political interests of a nation.

International law functions in the midst of a complex international political system. Conflicts are common. No worldwide central authority exists to enforce its rules or decisions. What is achieved comes about through the consent of countries based on their own political interests. International law's failures can be traced to the same source.

For Discussion

1. What are four main sources of international law? Describe them.
2. How do international politics affect international law?

Law of the Sea

Five hundred years ago, Spain and Portugal signed an agreement governing the world's oceans for all time. As the world's greatest maritime powers, they decided to divide the oceans between them. Under the authority of Pope Alexander VI, they drew a line on the globe: Spain claimed the Pacific Ocean, the Gulf of Mexico, and part of the Atlantic. Portugal got the Indian Ocean and the rest of the Atlantic. Any ships of other countries would have to seek permission to sail or be treated as trespassers.

This self-serving agreement was almost immediately challenged. Hugo Grotius, a Dutch scholar and lawyer working for the Dutch East India Company, wrote a book called *Mare Liberium* (*The Free Sea*) in 1609. In it he argued that the world's oceans should be accessible to all countries. Furthermore, he argued that countries claiming the right to travel and trade on the open seas could use force, if necessary, to protect this right. Other writers also made contributions to the idea of freedom of the seas. One, Cornelius Van Bynkershock, came up with what is often called the three-mile rule. He claimed that a state's right to control the sea ended within the three miles of its shoreline. He based his idea on the fact that 17th-century cannons had a range of three miles, giving a state that much effective control of coastal waters.

Eventually, the position of the these writers prevailed. Backed by the growing naval strength of the Netherlands and Great Britain, Spain and Portugal were forced to give up their scheme for ocean supremacy. The doctrine of freedom of the seas, first stated in the 17th century, became a basic part of international law.

Modern Developments

During the 20th century, new controversies arose about the law of the sea. The three-mile rule was challenged by nations seeking to extend their control over fishing waters and maritime rights. Limits of 12 miles and over 200 miles were claimed. Although it had long been agreed that the sea cannot be claimed in the same way as land, it became clear that if the nations of the world (many of them landlocked) all wished to use the sea, new agreements must be made for the mutual benefit of all nations and of the ocean itself.

Efforts to make these agreements took many years. They began under the League of Nations. Then, in 1958, the first U.N. conference on the law of the sea took place. Though some progress was made, the 1958 conventions failed to establish a universal body of maritime law.

In 1960, a second conference took place, but it too failed. It appeared that the use of the ocean would become a free-for-all, with countries pursuing conflicting goals.

In 1974, the Third U.N. Law of the Sea Convention assembled. Despite past failures, the U.N. General Assembly asked the convention to come up with a new, comprehensive plan for maritime use. To begin, the convention had to define what was meant by the "sea." It decided that the "sea" means oceans, gulfs, bays, and seas, but it does not mean rivers and lakes.

The resolution of other issues was more difficult. Where can a nation sail its ships? What rules must it follow to avoid harming the environment of other states and of the ocean itself? Can one nation prevent another from using parts of the sea near the nation? Can one nation pass through the straits over which another nation exercises sovereignty? Who can mine or fish in different parts of the sea? What rules are to govern the high seas and the international seabed?

The work of the conference went on for seven years. Various drafts of the new law of the sea were debated before the final version emerged.

The United States opposed provisions affecting seabed mining in the final version, but in April 1982, the conference adopted the text. One hundred thirty nations voted for it, four against it (including the United States), and 17 abstained. In spite of U.S. objections, the treaty became law in 1994 after 60 nations had ratified it. There are now 148 parties to the treaty, and its provisions may bind even non-parties, including the United States, as a matter of customary international law.

This 320-article, 200-page agreement covers just about every conceivable use of the sea. Each coastal nation can exercise its sovereignty over the sea adjacent to its coast, but the distance of that "belt of sea" had long been in dispute. The convention established 12 nautical miles as the maximum.

The convention defined rights of coastal states to the use of the continental shelf adjacent to their coasts, and it defined duties for coastal states as well. For instance, a nation has the right to authorize oil drilling, but also has a duty to establish environmental standards for all activities under its jurisdiction. These standards must meet international criteria.

Coastal states obtained new rights under the convention to establish an exclusive "economic zone" extending up to 200 miles from the coast. Within this 200-mile belt, a coastal state may, for instance, declare exclusive rights to explore and exploit the natural resources, to construct artificial islands for economic purposes, and to use the current or winds for energy production. It may also board ships in that zone when it has reason to believe that the ship is illegally discharging pollutants into the sea.

Other states, though, have the right to use any state's economic zone for certain purposes. For instance, any ship may sail through these waters and airplanes may fly over the area.

The convention laid down stronger safety and environmental rules for the high seas and coastal areas. All nations, for example, are free to fish on the high seas, but must follow conservation rules.

The convention also specifies duties that apply to most of the sea. Nations must protect the environment, promote marine studies, and protect archaeological treasures that might be found. Also, nations must use the seas for peaceful purposes and settle disputes peacefully. All states are required to have "due regard" for the rights of other states, and the spirit of cooperativeness is mandatory.

For Discussion

1. What does "freedom of the seas" mean? What has been the major debate over this freedom?
2. What other issues did the Law of the Sea Convention address?
3. Why do you think it was so difficult for this convention to get adopted?
4. Some philosophers maintain that the sea itself, or the inhabitants of the sea, have interests that must be taken into account. Do you agree with this position? Why or why not? If you were drafting a sea treaty, what provisions might you include to ensure that the sea and all the life within it were protected for their own sake, not just as resources for humanity?

Piracy

A U.S. Navy ship follows a suspected pirate vessel in the Indian Ocean.

When you think of pirates, you may imagine sailing ships, skull-and-crossbones flags, cutlasses, and colorful language: "Arghhhh," "Shiver me timbers," and "Ahoy, matey." The lore of pirates can be found in literature, folktales, and movies, but pirates also have a historical basis. In fact, the history of piracy can be traced back to the era of the ancient Mediterranean civilizations. The Phoenicians, Greeks, Romans and Carthaginians all indulged in piracy at different times.

In modern times, the late 17th and early 18th centuries might be considered the golden age of piracy. Numerous pirate bands raided ports and shipping in the Caribbean and along the North American coast. Legendary pirates such a William Kidd, Edward Teach (Blackbeard), Henry Morgan, Bartholomew Roberts (Black Bart), and Anne Bonney roamed the sea capturing merchant ships and their cargo. In spite of the romance and legend that has grown up around pirates, their actions spelled death and economic ruin for many innocent people, and many of the pirates themselves died violently or were hanged.

Because pirates operated on the open seas, they posed a special problem for the law. There was no international body to track them down, capture them, or put them on trial. Early on, rules developed for dealing with pirates. Piracy came to be considered a violation against the law of nations, all ships had the authority to attack pirates and bring them to justice under their own nation's laws. Usually the captured pirates were returned to a port, put on trial, and executed. Some pirates did not even receive a decent burial, but instead their rotting bodies or severed heads were displayed as a warning to other would-be pirates. Under certain circumstances, the law did not even require a trial. Some countries permitted summary execution of pirates captured on the high seas.

The problem of piracy has never gone away. Pirates still operate in many areas of the world including along the eastern coastline of Somalia, in the waters off Indonesia, off the coast bordering Nigeria, and in the Persian Gulf near Iran. Though their methods have changed, pirates still pose a serious threat to commerce and human lives. Today, a small group of pirates is most likely to use a motor-powered boat and be armed with small arms such as pistols, machetes, and automatic weapons. Once a vessel is boarded, pirates overpower the crew and steal what valuables and cargo they can easily take away. Sometimes, they will also kidnap crew members hoping to ransom them back to the shipping companies that employ them.

The modern law of piracy was established at the Law of the Sea Conventions of 1958 and 1982. It defines piracy as the seizure of a private ship on the high seas by violent means or illegally detaining persons or property aboard the seized ship for private gain. It also applies to private aircraft flying over international waters. Some have argued that the law is too narrow and needs to be changed to address modern conditions.

First of all, because territorial waters were expanded to 12 miles and modern pirates use small boats, many attacks on vessels do not take place in international waters. Such acts cannot be prosecuted as piracy.

Second, the modern law of piracy makes it clear that the motive of the pirate's act must be private gain. Thus the current law does not apply to groups working for governments or terrorists who are furthering their cause. Neither is working for private gain.

The International Maritime Bureau, an office of the International Chamber of Commerce in charge of monitoring the problem of piracy around the world, has proposed a new piracy law. It would define piracy as using or threatening force to board a ship in order to steal or commit another crime.

Supporters of the change argue that the law would address how pirates operate today. No longer could pirates avoid prosecution if they happened to seize a ship belonging to a government or if their motive was not private gain. Also, it would not matter whether the ship was seized in territorial or international waters.

Others worry that the proposed change goes too far. They argue that most crimes committed on the sea can be prosecuted anyway. For example, the Palestinian terrorists who hijacked the Italian cruise ship *Achille Lauro* in Egyptian territorial waters and killed an American passenger for political reasons were convicted of crimes related to the hijacking and murder. They also worry that governments could be charged with piracy if they try to legitimately seize a ship on the high seas.

Whether changes to the international law of piracy will be made remains to be seen. But the debate illustrates that piracy remains an important problem facing the international community and its law of the seas.

For Discussion

1. Why is piracy still a problem for the world community and international law?

2. How do modern pirates operate? Why might this present problems for prosecuting them under international piracy laws?

ACTIVITY

International Commission

Imagine that you are a delegate to an international commission convened to make recommendations about whether to adopt a new international definition of piracy. The proposed law has three significant clauses:

1. Crimes of piracy can be committed against private citizens and property and against personnel and property of sovereign states.

2. Crimes of piracy can be committed in both international and territorial waters excluding harbors, rivers, estuaries, and lakes.

3. Crimes of piracy can be committed for private gain or political purposes.

As a group, do the following for each clause:

1. Discuss these questions:

    a. What is the purpose of the clause?

    b. What are its pros?

    c. What are its cons?

2. Decide whether to recommend supporting or opposing the clause.

3. Be prepared to report your decisions and your reasons for them.

A Treaty to Control the Spread of Nuclear Weapons

"Fat Man" was the code name for the atomic bomb dropped on Nagasaki, Japan, in 1945.

At the end of World War II, the United States alone possessed atomic weapons. In 1949, however, the Soviet Union tested its first atomic bomb. This set off a nuclear-arms race with the United States lasting 40 years. Each country eventually produced more than 30,000 nuclear bombs and missile warheads.

Other nations also became nuclear powers. In 1952, Great Britain exploded its first atomic bomb. In 1960, France tested a nuclear device, and in 1964 China followed suit. All kept adding nuclear weapons to their arsenals.

The Non-Proliferation Treaty (NPT)

The Cuban Missile Crisis of 1962 nearly resulted in nuclear war between United States and the Soviet Union. The following year, the two superpowers, along with Britain, made the first attempt to control nuclear-arms development. The three nuclear nations signed a treaty promising not to test atomic weapons in the atmosphere or on land. But the treaty still permitted underground testing.

After China tested its first atomic device in 1964, the nuclear powers began negotiations that finally resulted in the Non-Proliferation Treaty of 1968. It took effect on March 5, 1970. The NPT has three main pillars: It strives to (1) stop the spread of nuclear weapons, (2) promote nuclear disarmament, and (3) assure the peaceful use of nuclear technology. NPT takes the form of promises between those nations already possessing nuclear weapons and those nations without them.

Those nations possessing nuclear weapons promise to:

1. Not help nations without nuclear weapons acquire or develop them.
2. Place security safeguards on their nuclear materials and technology to prevent their export to nations without nuclear weapons.
3. Share nuclear technology for peaceful purposes with all treaty members.
4. Work to end the nuclear-arms race and reduce their nuclear-weapons stockpiles.

Those nations not possessing nuclear weapons promise to:

1. Not acquire or develop nuclear weapons.
2. Accept security safeguards, including U.N. inspections, on all domestically produced or imported nuclear materials and technology to assure they are not being used for military purposes.
3. Place security safeguards on their nuclear materials and technology to prevent prohibited exports to other nations without nuclear weapons.
4. Share nuclear technology for peaceful purposes with all treaty members.

Today, almost every country in the world, including all five original nuclear powers, have signed the Non-Proliferation Treaty. Only four nations are not part of the treaty—India, Pakistan, North Korea, and Israel. All of these four except Israel have confirmed that they have developed nuclear weapons. Israel is widely suspected of having nuclear weapons.

NPT member nations without nuclear weapons must agree to accept the system of safeguards and inspections of the International Atomic Energy Agency. This independent U.N. agency requires two things from non-nuclear nations. First, they must declare what nuclear materials and equipment they possess. Second, they must submit to regular inspections to make sure nothing they possess is being diverted to weapons development. Most of the treaty members that possess nuclear weapons have also agreed to observe strict security safeguards on exports of nuclear material.

The Breakup of the Soviet Union

The breakup of the Soviet Union into 15 independent nations in 1991 brought an end to the 40-year nuclear-arms race of the Cold War. The Start II Treaty of 1993 between the United States and Russia greatly reduced the number of nuclear warheads in both countries. The following year, the two powers agreed to stop targeting each other's territory with ballistic missiles. The former Cold War adversaries also declared a suspension of all forms of nuclear testing.

But there was a negative side to the Soviet breakup. Nuclear missiles capable of reaching the United States still existed in Russia. (The former Soviet Republics of Belarus, Kazakhstan, and Ukraine also possessed nuclear weapons, but they destroyed or transported them to Russia in the 1990s). The United States worried that Russia could not effectively keep its nuclear material and technology secure from improper exports or even smuggling. Also troubling was the potential emigration of former Soviet scientists to nations seeking to develop nuclear weapons. To help address these issues, the U.S. Congress granted $800 million in aid to help the former Soviet states "denuclearize."

Iraq

Following the Persian Gulf War in 1991, U.N. inspectors discovered that Iraq had established a massive nuclear-weapons program. It was only a few years away from producing an atomic bomb. Even more shocking, Iraq had signed the Non-Proliferation Treaty. It had proceeded with a secret nuclear program even though NPT safeguards were in place and inspections were occurring. Iraq had been illegally importing nuclear materials and equipment for years from Western nations, including the United States.

The United Nations instituted widespread inspections of Iraqi installations and strengthened safeguards preventing international trade in nuclear materials and technology. This seemed to put the Non-Proliferation Treaty back on track. But in 1998, Iraq's leader, Saddam Hussein, refused to permit U.N. inspectors into certain areas. In response, the U.N. removed its inspectors from Iraq, and the United States and Great Britain carried out bombing raids on suspected nuclear facilities. Iraq's actions contributed to the decision of the United States, Great Britain, and other nations to invade Iraq in 2003. The resulting war and occupation effectively ended fears of a Iraqi nuclear-weapons program, but no nuclear weapons or programs were discovered.

North Korea

The Korean peninsula is divided into South Korea and Communist North Korea. From 1950 to 1953, war raged between North and South, with Chinese troops aiding the North and U.S. troops (acting on behalf of the United Nations) helping the South. Nearly 30,000 American troops remain stationed in South Korea.

North Korea signed the Non-Proliferation Treaty in 1986, but delayed agreeing to required inspections and other safeguards on its nuclear program. Negotiations among the United States, South Korea, and North Korea ended with an agreement in 1991 making the entire Korean peninsula a nuclear weapons-free zone.

U.S. President George W. Bush and Russian President Vladimir Putin sign a nuclear-arms reduction treaty in Moscow on May 24, 2002.

In 1992, North Korea signed an agreement allowing U.N. inspections of its nuclear facilities, which had been suspected of producing materials for nuclear weapons. But when the inspectors arrived, North Korea denied them access to some installations. Meanwhile, satellite pictures revealed evidence of continued nuclear-weapons development. In 1993, North Korea withdrew from the Non-Proliferation Treaty, but then quickly suspended its withdrawal.

Seeing the threat posed by North Korea, the United States moved additional troops into Asia in 1994. In a final effort to avoid a crisis, the Clinton administration sent former President Jimmy Carter to North Korea. The two sides reached an agreement. In exchange for the North Koreans freezing their nuclear-weapons program and agreeing to international inspections, the Americans promised to cooperate in helping the country obtain nuclear-power plants. But four years later, the United States detected the North Koreans constructing a huge new underground nuclear complex. The famine-plagued Communist country then demanded massive food shipments before it would allow inspections of this underground facility. In March 1999, the Clinton administration agreed to give North Korea $60 million in food assistance.

The Clinton administration continued to negotiate with North Korea. The new Bush administration, however, decided against direct negotiations, saying that it refused to reward North Korea's bad behavior. In 2002, it detected a North Korean uranium-processing program in violation of the 1994 agreement and stopped shipments of oil promised in the 1994 agreement. In response, North Korea started up a nuclear facility it had shut down since 1994, ordered nuclear inspectors out of the country, and announced in 2003 its withdrawal from the NPT. In that same year, the North Korean government claimed to possess nuclear weapons and began testing long-range missile delivery systems. Six-party talks began between the United States, North Korea, South Korea, China, Russia, and Japan. In October 2006, North Korea tested its first nuclear weapon. Four months later, a tentative agreement was reached. In return for receiving $400 million in aid, North Korea agreed to shut down its nuclear facility again and allow nuclear inspectors back in the country. The talks continue.

India and Pakistan

When India gained its independence in 1947 from Great Britain, it was carved into two countries—India, with a mostly Hindu population, and Pakistan, with an overwhelmingly Muslim population. The two South Asian countries have never gotten along well. They have already fought three conventional wars and almost fought a fourth in 1990. Hindu-Muslim religious hatreds continue to fuel longstanding border disputes. Currently, the two countries are engaging in a regional nuclear-arms race. Neither country has signed the Non-Proliferation Treaty, but both have agreed not to attack each other's nuclear installations.

India exploded its first nuclear device in 1974. When India conducted new nuclear tests in May 1998, Pakistan followed with its first test explosions. In April 1999, India and then Pakistan tested missiles that could hurl nuclear warheads deep inside each other's territory.

Unlike the United States and Soviet Union during the Cold War, India and Pakistan are next door to one another, making missile flight times extremely short. Neither country has the careful controls that the Americans and Soviets developed to prevent accidental missile launchings.

The United States imposed trade and economic-aid restrictions on both nations after the round of nuclear tests in 1998.

In March 2006, the United States announced an agreement with India. The United States will provide India with civilian nuclear technology. In return, India agreed to allow inspectors to look at its civilian nuclear program. This agreement drew criticism because India refuses to sign the NPT, and the new technology will probably enable India to produce more nuclear material for its military program. The Bush administration defends the agreement because of India's commitment to democracy and because India for the first time is permitting nuclear inspectors to enter the country.

Iran

In the 1950s and '60s, the United States aided Iran, then under the control of Shah Mohammad Reza Pahlavi, to develop a nuclear-energy program. In 1970, Iran ratified the NPT. The cooperation between the two countries lasted until the overthrow of the Shah's regime in 1979. The new Iranian government was led by the radical Islamic cleric Ayatolla Khomeini.

Judging the new regime to be too unstable, the United States and various European countries stopped all nuclear aid to Iran. After the revolution, Iran decided to restart its nuclear-energy program using fuel processed locally. In the 1990s, Iran began to explore ways to enrich uranium, a process that could produce material for nuclear weapons. In 2002, it was revealed that Iran was operating two previously unknown nuclear sites, and in 2006 Iran announced that it had successfully enriched uranium. It, however, restated its claim that its goal is not the production of nuclear weapons, but rather the production of power for domestic use.

The enrichment of uranium itself is not prohibited under the NPT, and the development of nuclear energy by all countries is permitted. But the United States and other Western countries worry about Iranian motives. Iran has promoted Islamist causes throughout the Middle East and is accused of supplying conventional weapons to radical groups such as Hezbollah. The fear that Iran could develop nuclear weapons and in the future provide them to terrorists or Islamist revolutionaries has led the United States and other countries to call for the U.N. Security Council to impose sanctions to halt Iranian nuclear ambitions.

Is the NPT Working?

Although North Korea, India and Pakistan, and Iran offer significant challenges to the goals of non-proliferation, most of the world's nations today have rejected atomic weapons. In 1995, 178 nations agreed to extend the NPT indefinitely. The next year, most nations in the world, including the United States, signed a treaty banning all tests of nuclear weapons.

Still problems remain. As demonstrated by North Korea, a country that wants to develop a nuclear-weapons capacity can do so by withdrawing from the treaty and resisting international pressure to conform. And as shown by Iran, it is difficult to measure and judge the real motivations of governments that claim to be developing nuclear resources for peaceful means, but may be trying to develop nuclear arms.

For Discussion

1. What is the purpose of the Non-Proliferation Treaty? How is it enforced?
2. How did the breakup of the Soviet Union both strengthen and weaken efforts to control the proliferation of nuclear weapons in the world?
3. Which of the nations currently developing nuclear weapons do you think poses the greatest threat to the United States? Why?

ACTIVITY

Next Steps

In this activity, students decide which area presents the most danger and recommend steps the United States should take to reduce the danger of nuclear war in this area.

As a group, do the following:

1. Review these four areas: (1) Russia, Belarus, Kazakhstan, and Ukraine; (2) Iran; (3) North Korea; and (4) India and Pakistan.
2. Decide which area presents the most danger of nuclear war and why.
3. Make recommendations on what the United States should do to reduce the danger of nuclear war.
4. Present your decision and recommendations to the rest of the class.

Bibliography

Unit 1: Sir Edward Coke and the Common Law

Bowen, Catherine Drinker. *The Lion and the Throne: The Life and Times of Sir Edward Coke.* Boston: Little, Brown and Company, 1956.

Boyer, Allen D. *Sir Edward Coke and the Elizabethan Age.* Stanford, Calif.: Stanford University Press, 2003.

Caenegem, R.C. van. *The Birth of the English Common Law.* Second Edition. Cambridge: Cambridge University Press, 1988.

Coote, Stephen. *A Play of Passion: The Life of Sir Walter Ralegh.* London: Macmillan London Ltd., 1993.

Cosgrove, Richard A. *Scholars of the Law: English Jurisprudence from Blackstone to Hart.* New York: New York University Press, 1996.

Encyclopaedia Britannica. Articles titled "Adversary Procedure," "Charles I," "Common Law," "Edward I," "Henry De Bracton," "James I," "Jury," "Sir Edward Coke," "Henry II," "Petition of Right," "Sir William Blackstone," and "United Kingdom." Online Edition. Accessed March 2006. URL: www.britannica.com

Knafla, Louis A. *Law and Politics in Jacobean England: The Tracts of Lord Chancellor Ellesmere.* London: Cambridge University Press, 1977.

Seagle, William. *Men of Law: From Hammurabi to Holmes.* Chapters titled "Edward Plantagenet: The Scheme, Mold, and Model of Common Law," "Thomas Egerton, Baron Ellesmere and Viscount Brackley: The Keeping of the King's Conscience," "Sir Edward Coke, and His Lady of the Common Law," "Sir William Blackstone: Law and Popularization," and "Jeremy Bentham: The Vanity of Law Reform." New York: Hafner Publishing Co., 1971.

___. *The History of Law.* Chapters titled "The Rise of Legal Systems" and "The Quest for Equity." New York: Tudor Publishing Co., 1949.

White, Stephen D. *Sir Edward Coke and "The Grievances of the Commonwealth," 1621-1628.* Chapel Hill: University of North Carolina Press, 1979.

Winston, John. *Sir Walter Ralegh.* London: Michael Joseph Ltd., 1975.

Wormser, Rene A. *The Story of the Law and the Men Who Made It–From the Earliest Times to the Present.* Part titled "The English." New York: Simon and Schuster, 1962.

Zane, John Maxcy. *The Story of Law.* Chapters titled "The Origins of English Law," "English Law–Righteous and Unrighteous," and "The Reconciliation of the English System of Law." Second Edition. Indianapolis: Liberty Fund, 1998.

Unit 2: The Enlightenment Philosophers

Cassirer, Ernst. *The Philosophy of the Enlightenment.* Princeton: Princeton University Press, 1968.

Conroy, Peter V. *Jean-Jacques Rousseau.* New York: Twayne Publishers, 1998.

Encyclopaedia Britannica. Articles titled "Charles-Louis de Secondat, baron de La Brede et Montesquieu," "Enlightenment," "History of Science," "Thomas Hobbes," "John Locke," and "Jean-Jacques Rousseau." Online Edition. Accessed March 2006. URL: www.britannica.com

Hobbes, Thomas. *Leviathan.* London: Penguin Classics, 1982.

Levine, Andrew. *Engaging Political Philosophy from Hobbes to Rawls.* Oxford: Blackwell Publishers, 2002.

Locke, John. *The Selected Political Writings of John Locke.* New York: W.W. Norton, 2005.

___. *Two Treatises of Government.* New Haven ; Yale University Press, 2003.

Montesquieu, Charles de. Montesquieu: The Spirit of the Laws. Cambridge, UK: Cambridge University Press, 1989.

Rousseau, Jean-Jacques, translated by Maurice Cranston. *The Social Contract.* London: Penguin Classics, 1968.

Wormser, Rene A. *The Story of the Law and the Men Who Made It–From the Earliest Times to the Present.* Chapters titled "Five Reformers" and "Hobbes and Locke." New York: Simon and Schuster, 1962.

Yolton, John W. *The Two Intellectual Worlds of John Locke: Man, Person, and Spirits in the Essay.* Ithaca, N.Y.: Cornell University Press, 2004.

Unit 3: The Code Napoleon

Caenegem, R. C. van. *European Law in the Past and the Future.* New York: Cambridge University Press, 2002.

David, Rene and Henry P. de Vries. *The French Legal System: An Introduction to the Civil Law System.* New York: Oceana Publications, 1958.

Diamond, John L., Lawrence C. Levine, M., and M. Stuart Madden. *Understanding Torts.* New York: Matthew Bender & Co., 1999.

Encyclopaedia Britannica. Articles titled "Civil Law," "French Revolution," "France," "Louis XVI," "Napoleon I," "Napoleonic Code," and "Voltaire." Online Edition. Accessed March 2006. URL: www.britannica.com

Holmberg, Tom. "The Origins of the Code: An Overview." *Napoleon Series.* URL: http://www.napoleon-series.org

Schwartz, Bernard. *The Code Napoleon and the Common-Law World.* New York: New York University Press, 1956.

Seagle, William. *The History of Law.* Chapter titled "The Age of Codification." New York: Tudor Publishing Co., 1949.

Spence, George, translator. *The Code Napoleon, Or, the French Civil Code.* London: The Lawbook Exchange, 2004.

Wormser, Rene A. *The Story of the Law and the Men Who Made It–From the Earliest Times to the Present.* Chapter titled "Napoleon." New York: Simon and Schuster, 1962.

Unit 4: The Dreyfus Affair

Bredin, Jean-Denis. *The Affair: The Case of Alfred Dreyfus.* New York: G. Braziller, 1986.

Burns, Michael. *France and the Dreyfus Affair: A Documentary History.* Boston: Bedford/St. Martins, 1999.

Derfler, Leslie. *The Dreyfus Affair.* Westport, Conn.: Greenwood Press, 2002.

Encyclopaedia Britannica. Articles titled "Alfred Dreyfus," "Devils Island," "Emile Zola," "France," and "Georges Clemenceau." Online Edition. Accessed March 2006. URL: www.britannica.com

Franklin, Charles. *World-Famous Trials: The Conflict and Drama of History's Greatest Court-Room Classics.* New York: Taplinger Publishing Company, 1966.

Hoffman, Robert L. *More Than a Trial.* New York: Free Press, 1980.

Johnson, Martin Phillip. *The Dreyfus Affair.* New York: St. Martin's Press, 1999.

Kleeblatt, Norman, ed. *The Dreyfus Affair, Art, Truth, and Justice.* Berkeley, Calif.: University of California Press, 1987.

Raby, R. Cornelius. *Fifty Famous Trials.* Washington, D.C.: Washington Law Book Co., 1937.

Snyder, Louis Leo. *The Dreyfus Case: A Documentary History.* New Brunswick, N.J.: Rutgers University Press, 1973.

Whyte, George R. *The Dreyfus Affair: A Chronological History.* New York: Palgrave Macmillan, 2005.

Unit 5: The Totalitarians

Broszat, Martin translated by John W. Hiden. *The Hitler State: The Foundation and Development of the Internal Structure of the Third Reich.* New York: Longman, 1981.

Burleigh, Michael. *The Third Reich: A New History.* New York: Hill and Wang, 2000.

Conquest, Robert. *The Great Terror: A Reassessment.* New York: Oxford University Press, 1990.

De Jong, Alex. *Stalin and the Shaping of the Soviet Union.* New York: William Morrow, 1986.

Encyclopaedia Britannica. Articles titled "Adolf Hitler," "Erwin Rommel," "Germany," "Heinrich Himmler," "Joseph Stalin," "Leon Trotsky," "Purge Trials," "Reichstag Fire," "Russia," "Russian Revolution of 1917," "Sergey Mironovich Kirov," "Soviet Law," "Totalitarianism," and "Vladimir Ilich Lenin." Online Edition. Accessed March 2006. URL: www.britannica.com

Fest, Joachim C. translated by Bruce Little. *Plotting Hitler's Death: The Story of the German Resistance.* New York: Henry Holt, 1996.

Fischer, Klaus P. *Nazi Germany: A New History.* New York: Continuum, 1995.

Forman, James D. *Code Name Valkyrie: Count von Stauffenberg and the Plot to Kill Hitler.* New York: S.G. Phillips, 1973.

Müller, Ingo translated by Deborah Lucas Schneider. *Hitler's Justice: The Courts of the Third Reich.* Cambridge, Mass.: Harvard University Press, 1991.

Tucker, Robert C. *Stalin in Power: The Revolution from Above, 1928-1941.* New York: W.W. Norton & Company, 1990.

Medvedev, Roy. *Let History Judge.* New York: Columbia University Press, 1989.

Unit 6: War Crimes

Conot, Robert E. *Justice at Nuremberg.* New York: Harper & Row, 1983.

Encyclopaedia Britannica. Articles titled "Adolf Hitler," "Nürnberg Trials," and "War Crime." Online Edition. Accessed March 2006. URL: www.britannica.com

Horvitz, Leslie Alan. *Encyclopedia of War Crimes and Genocide.* New York: Facts on File, 2006.

Mann, Abby. *Judgment at Nuremberg.* New York: New Directions, 2002.

McGoldrick Dominic, Peter Rowe, and Eric Donnelly, editors. *The Permanent International Criminal Court: Legal and Policy Issues.* Portland, Or.: Hart Pub., 2004.

Meron, Theodor. *War Crimes Law Comes of Age: Essays.* New York: Oxford University Press, 1998.

Mettraux, Guenael. *International Crimes and the Ad Hoc Tribunals.* New York: Oxford University Press, 2006.

"Trials of War Criminals." *Encyclopedia of the Holocaust.* Vol. 4. New York: Macmillan, 1990.

Watkins, John C. *War Crimes and War Crime Trials: From Leipzig to the ICC and Beyond: Cases, Materials and Comments.* Durham, N.C.: Carolina Academic Press, 2006.

Unit 7: Gandhi and Civil Disobedience

Attenborough, Richard, comp. *The Words of Gandhi.* New York: Newmarket Press, 1982.

Chadha, Yogesh. *Gandhi, A Life.* New York: John Wiley & Sons, 1997.

Encyclopaedia Britannica. Articles titled "Civil Disobedience," "India," "Mohandas Karamchand Gandhi," and "United Kingdom." Online Edition. Accessed March 2006. URL: www.britannica.com

Gandhi, Mahatma. *Selected Writings of Mahatma Gandhi.* Boston: Beacon, 1951.

Gardner, Howard. *Extraordinary Minds: Portraits of Exceptional Individuals and an Examination of Our Extraordinariness.* New York: Basic Books, 1997.

Judd, Denis. *The Lion and the Tiger: the Rise and Fall of the British Raj, 1600-1947.* New York: Oxford University Press, 2004.

Parekh, Bhikhu C. *Gandhi: A Very Short Introduction.* New York: Oxford University Press, 2001.

Raja Rao. *The Great Indian Way: A Life of Mahatma Gandhi.* New Delhi: Vision Books, 1998.

Walsh, Judith E. *A Brief History of India.* New York: Facts on File, 2006.

Wolpert, Stanley A. *Gandhi's Passion: The Life and Legacy of Mahatma Gandhi.* New York: Oxford University Press, 2001.

Unit 8: International Law

Aust, Anthony. *Handbook of International Law.* Cambridge, UK: Cambridge University Press, 2005.

Brownlie, Ian. *Principles of Public International Law.* Fifth Edition. Oxford, UK: Clarendon Press, 1998.

Cooper, Matthew. "A Nuclear Deal." *Time* 13 Mar. 2006.

Doyle, Mark. "Somali piracy is worst in world." BBC News. Accessed August 2006. URL: news.bbc.co.uk

Encyclopaedia Britannica. Articles titled "International Agreement," "International Law," "Ship," and "Treaty." Online Edition. Accessed March 2006. URL: www.britannica.com

Fonte, John. "The Ideological War Within the West." *Watch on the West.* Vol. 3, No. 6, May 2002. Accessed August 2006. URL: www.amasci.com

Gardner, Gary T. *Nuclear Nonproliferation, A Primer.* Boulder, Colo.: Lynne Rienner Pub., 1994.

Gutoff, Jonathan M. "The Law of Piracy in Popular Culture." *Journal of Maritime Law & Commerce.* Vol. 31, No. 4. October 2000.

Hallinan, Conn. "Nuclear Proliferation: A Gathering Storm." Foreign Policy in Focus. Accessed August 2006. URL: www.fpif.org

Hirsh, Michael and Barry, John. "Nuclear Jitters." *Newsweek.* 8 June 1998.

Hirsch, Michael, Melinda Liu, and George Wehfritz. "A Regime's Nuclear Secrets." *Newsweek*. 23 Oct. 2006.

"IMB releases latest piracy statistics." International Chamber of Commerce. Accessed August 2006. URL: www.icc-ccs.org

Kirgis, Frederic L. "North Korea's Withdrawal From the Nuclear Nonproliferation Treaty. January 2003. American Society of International Law. Accessed August 2006. URL: www.asil.org

Macleod/Havana, Scott. "A Date with a Dangerous Mind." *Time*. 25 Sept. 2006.

McGeary, Johanna. "Will This Man Get the Bomb?" *Time*. 3 Apr. 2006.

"Nuclear Weapons Program—North Korea." Accessed August 2006. URL: www.fas.org

Paquete Habana and the *Lola*, 175 U.S. 677, 1900.

"Piracy attacks drop in 2005—International Maritime Bureau." AFX News Limited. Accessed August 2006. URL: www.forbes.com

"Piracy, Then & Now." Accessed August 2006. URL: blinkdat.hegewisch.net/pirates/piracy.html

Powell, Bill. "When Outlaws Get the Bomb." *Time*. 23 Oct. 2006.

Scott, Shirley V. *International Law in World Politics*. Boulder, Colo.: Lynne Rienner Publishers, 2004.

"Timeline: North Korea's nuclear weapons development." 6 January 2004. Accessed August 2006. URL: www.cnn.com

"Treaty on the Non-Proliferation of Nuclear Weapons." U.S. Department of State. Accessed August 2006. URL: www.state.gov

Vallar, Cindy. "Piracy and the Law." Accessed August 2006. URL: www.cindyvallar.com

Wikipedia. Articles titled "North Korea and Weapons of Mass Destruction," "Nuclear Non-Proliferation Treaty," "Nuclear Program of Iran," Accessed August 2006. URL: en.wikipedia.org

Photo Credits

Photographs and illustrations reprinted with the permission of the following:

AP Images: p. 106

Corbis: pp. 73, 82, 85

Evgeny Gerashchenko: p. 75

Hulton-Deutsch Collections/Corbis: p. 80

ICC-CPI/Wim Van Cappellen: p. 96

iStockphoto.com: cover 7 (Jeremy Edwards); p. 28 (Bora Ucak); p. 55 (Joachim Angeltum); cover 6, p. 100 (Vazhappully Bahastcaran Baiju); p. 108 (Klass Lingbeek-Van Kramen); p. 114 (Allan Morrison)

Public domain photographs and illustrations from the following:

Images of American Political History: p. 94

Library of Congress: cover 3; pp. 12, 27, 32, 44, 66

U.S. National Archives & Records Administration: p. 78

U.S. Navy: p. 116

White House: p. 120

Wikimedia Commons: cover 1, 4, 5; pp. 6, 11, 14, 17, 37, 40, 47, 58, 70, 90, 103, 118

Wikipedia: cover 2; pp. 9, 21, 30, 35, 87 (Adam Carr), 111